CONFLICT RESOLUTION

PEACE IMPLEMENTATION IN NEW WARS

MELANIE FLOWERS

CONFLICT RESOLUTION

PEACE IMPLEMENTATION IN NEW WARS

MELANIE FLOWERS

Flowers Publications
Flowers School of Technology and Management
Germany • United Kingdom

Flowers, Melanie
Conflict Resolution: Peace Implementation in New Wars | Melanie Flowers

ISBN-13: 978-1453653159 | ISBN-10: 1453653155

Conflict Resolution, Peace Implementation, Negotiation, Mediation.

Printed in the United States of America

www.flowers.de.com
www.flowersschool.com

TABLE OF CONTENTS

LIST OF FIGURES

LIST OF TABLES

LIST OF MAPS

LIST OF ABBREVIATIONS

ACS	American Colonization Society
AFL	Armed Forces of Liberia
AU	African Union
CDC	Congress for Democratic Change
COS	Council of State
CMC	Contract and Monopolies Commission
CRC-NPFL	Central Revolutionary Council – National Patriotic Front of Liberia
DR	Disarmament, Reintegration
DDRR	Disarmament, Demobilization, Reintegration, Rehabilitation
ECOMIL	Economic Community of West African States Mission in Liberia
ECOMOG	Economic Community of West African States Cease-Fire Monitoring Group
ECOWAS	Economic Community of West African States
EU	European Union
GEMAP	Liberia Governance and Economic Management Assistance Plan
GOL	Government of Liberia
GRC	Governance Reform Commission
HIPC	Heavily Indebted Poor Countries
IDP	Internally Displaced Person
IGNU	Interim Government of National Unity
IMC	International Monitoring Committee
ISF	International Stabilization Force
INPFL	Independent National Patriotic Front of Liberia
JMC	Joint Monitoring Committee
LDF	Lofa Defence Force
LNP	Liberian National Police
LNTG	Liberia National Transitional Government
LPC	Liberia Peace Council
LURD	Liberians United for Reconciliation and Democracy
MINUCI	United Nations Mission in Côte d'Ivoire
MODEL	Movement for Democracy in Liberia
NCDDRR	National Commission for Disarmament,

	Demobilization, Rehabilitation and Reintegration
NEC	National Elections Commission
NPFL	National Patriotic Front of Liberia
NPRA	National Patriotic Reconstruction Assembly
NPP	National Patriotic Party
NTGL	National Transitional Government of Liberia
OAU	Organization of African Unity
PRC	People's Redemption Council
RUF	Revolutionary United Front
SMC	Standing Mediation Committee
ULIMO	United Liberation Movement of Liberia for Democracy
ULIMO-J	ULIMO under Roosevelt Johnson
ULIMO-K	ULIMO under Alhaji Kromah
UN	United Nations
UNAMSIL	United Nations Mission in Sierra Leone
UNDP	United Nations Development Programme
UNMIL	United Nations Mission in Liberia
UNOL	United Nations Office in Liberia
UNOMIL	United Nations Observer Mission in Liberia
UNPOL	United Nations Police
UP	Unity Party

— To my grandmother Tamara Tiletzek who guided me throughout my personal and educational life.

— To my father Stephan Tiletzek for his incessant support throughout the ups and downs in my academic and life in general.

ACKNOWLEDGEMENTS

I would like to express my gratitude to my academic research mentors Professor Dr. Andreas Hasenclever and Dr. Thomas Nielebock, Institute of Political Science, Eberhard Karls University Tuebingen, for their guidance and constructive comments from the initial to the final stage of my research work, which forms the foundation for this publication. I would also like to thank Dr. Joseph K. Adonu, University of Bedfordshire, for his review and constructive criticism of the first draft of the work. Words cannot express my gratitude to my loving husband Michael Flowers for his tireless support and patience throughout my studies, for narrating and clarifying events surrounding the dynamics of the Liberian conflicts and for proofreading the work. This acknowledgement is incomplete without the mention of my deep indebtedness to my grandparents Hilda and Georg Schuy, Aline Mannseicher, and Edina Venezia for their support.

ONE

Introduction

The conditions[1] and required devices for moving conflict parties in civil wars to the signing of a peace agreement was the subject-matter of the conflict resolution and civil wars studies in the 1980s. It was assumed that a peace contract between the conflict parties would remain in effect after its signing and successful negotiations would bring about an irrevocable reduction of conflict[2]. However, the empirical outcome of peace processes of the 1990s and early 2000s shows that the linear approach to conflict resolution can no longer be upheld, and war actors often decide to return to war activities if no third party intervenes to verify or enforce the implementation of a peace agreement during the transition phase[3].

Furthermore, the "issues and preoccupations of the 21st century present new and often fundamentally different types of challenges [...] As new realities and challenges have emerged, so too have new expectations for action and new standards of conduct in national and international affairs"[4]. The features of new wars, such as, for example, the proliferation of private actors with divergent goals, and the criminalization of the war economy and the therewith connected internationalization of war-related activities, have consequences for the likelihood of a successful peace process in general and of a successful peace implementation in particular. Liberia's civil wars can, for

---

[1] For example, the ripeness of conflict as the precondition for peace negotiations – Zartman 1989.
[2] Stedman et al. 2002: 2.
[3] Walter 2002: 3.
[4] ICISS 2001: 3.

example, be characterized as new wars: the features of new wars can be identified, among others, the brutalization of war strategies, the privatization of war actors, and the criminalization of the war economy. Such new war characteristics contributed to a prolonged armed conflict, which could only be ended after favourable conditions were given or established and comprehensive provisions were set down and implemented during peace implementation. New types of challenges also require different kinds of responses and actors to tackle them: traditional peacekeeping operations were replaced by peacekeeping missions, that combine peacekeeping tasks with peacemaking and post-conflict peacebuilding components, and involve different kinds of actors (non-governmental organisations, sub-regional organisations, international organisations, regional powers and local actors, thereby combining local, regional and international third party levels).

The phase immediately following the signing of a peace agreement is very crucial for further progress as the peace process is susceptible to breaking down at such stage. As such, the rapid deployment of peacekeepers to the war-affected country and the timely setting up of an efficient and effective peacekeeping mission is a necessary precondition for the maintenance of the established cease fire and the implementation of the peace agreement provisions, as also reflected in the Brahimi Report, "[t]he first 6 to 12 weeks following a ceasefire or peace accord are often the most critical ones for establishing both a stable peace and the credibility of a new operation. Opportunities lost during that period are hard to regain."[5]

Several factors - security concerns of the former combatants and/or presence of spoilers - can be responsible for the breakdown of a peace process. Stedman (2001a/b), for example, differentiates 13 conflicts with respect to the difficulty of the conflict environment and the level of involvement of third parties in the implementation phase. Determinants such as the presence of spoilers and natural resources in a conflict require the intervention of a more involved and powerful third party with the appropriate means and strategies in order to yield a successful

---

[5] United Nations 2000: Brahimi-Report, xi.

peace implementation. In comparison to the attention given to the causes and durations of civil wars[6], and the determination of the ripe entry point to peace negotiations, the significance of a successful implementation phase[7] for the overall peace process of a particular armed conflict has received less attention in topic-related research.

The preceding elaborations highlight the challenges to contemporary peace processes, especially during the implementation phase of a peace agreement. The research work contributes knowledge to the understanding of the challenges to peace processes during peace implementation and identifies factors that are decisive or necessary for a successful peace implementation in the context of a new war. Thus, the overall research question can be phrased as follows: *Which factors condition the success or failure of a peace process in the implementation phase of a new war?*

Chapter Two specifies the concept of peace implementation: it introduces the term peace and differentiates between the broader concept peace consolidation from the more specific, narrowed down concept peace implementation. The chapter, further, presents a literature overview on the termination of civil wars, and the considered explanatory approaches are assessed in regard to the applicability of their identified success factors for war termination to the peace implementation phase.

In Chapter Three, the theoretical model and research hypotheses are derived, considering the preceding specifications of the concepts peace implementation and new wars, and the identified success factors for war termination in other research works. The theoretical model incorporates the assumptions of Rational Choice Theory: under certain conditions, opportunities and constraints, the involved actors select the course of action which seems to be the most advantageous in regard to the achievement of their goals. The chapter concludes with the

---

[6] The greed vs. grievance debate is concerned with the causes of civil wars; Fearon (2004) investigates, for example, why some civil wars last longer than others.
[7] The terms implementation phase, peace implementation phase, peace implementation and implementation of a peace are used as synonyms in this study and are used interchangeably. See Chapter Two for the definition of peace implementation.

selection of the research method and other methodical considerations.

Chapter Four applies the generated theoretical model and hypotheses to the three most significant peace implementation phases of the Liberia case study. First, an overview of the history and political background of Liberia's civil wars is presented. Liberia is then classified as a new war, before the peace agreements of Cotonou, Abuja and Accra are assessed in detail with respect to the respective value of the independent and dependent variables. The study then offers explanations as to why numerous peace agreements and associated implementation processes were required in order to end the conflict in Liberia.

The conclusion assesses the conducted research and its scope and limits of validity with respect to the chosen concepts, theoretical model and empirical study. The research work concludes with an outlook to possible future research.

TWO

Implementation of Peace Agreements in New Wars

Relevance and Specification of Research

The security situation is the most volatile immediately following the signing of a peace agreement, and there is a high level of risk for the conflict to break out again. This is generally the case as the violence does not often ebb down in all parts of the affected country during peace negotiations. Out of this reason, a successful peace implementation is vital for the stabilization of the peace process. It, on the other hand, does not guarantee the prevention of a renewed war or the rekindling of armed conflict, as long as no mid- and long-term peace consolidating measures have been put in place, to deal with or remove the underlying causes of the civil war and war-related consequences. Peace implementation can only lay the cornerstone for long-term peace. The concept of new wars provides important insights into the challenges for third parties and conflict parties to end a civil war that has the characteristics of a new war. In particular, the features of new wars are considered in the formulation of peace-implementing measures as they tend to have implications for the success prospects of a peace process. The aim of this work is to, first, show which strategies, peace agreement provisions and resulting measures are set down in the peace agreement of the chosen case study and to what extent they are implemented. Secondly, it assesses to what extent the features of new wars are therein considered (for example, the regulation of the trade in diamonds) and the effect this had on the overall implementation process. The study extends the scope of application of the concept of new wars as its utility and relevance for the explanation of successful or failed peace implementations is highlighted. In order to fully capturing the complexity of the termination of new wars, factors such as the emergence of private actors and the presence of valuable natural resources as an important source of finance for war activities were considered necessary for the analysis. As such factors are not sufficient in explaining success or failure of peace implementation, other supplemental determining parameters available in civil wars research (literature), such as provisions for power-sharing, are factored in the evolution of the theoretical model. The purpose of this research work is to generate a theory, which, firstly, contributes to the understanding of the challenges and success conditions for the termination of a new war in the implementation phase, and, secondly, through the consideration of given structures and conditions, which directly affect the key actors involved in a conflict, explain, why a peace agreement is implemented in case X and, a relapse to extended violence can occur in case Y.

The empirical part of the study covers the peace process in Liberia. There is little focus on the Liberian civil wars in literature as well as in the international media in comparison to, for example, the civil wars in Rwanda and Bosnia. Existing literature on the Liberian case mainly focuses on the role of the West African sub-regional organisation called ECOWAS (Economic Community of West African States) during the first Liberian civil war of 1989-1996 and the intervention of its ad-hoc formed peacekeeping force ECOMOG (Economic Community of West African States Monitoring Group). Other works are concerned only with aspects of the Liberian civil wars that relate to the emergence of warlords and the financing of war activities through the exploitation of and the trade in valuable natural resources (such as the trade in diamonds between Liberian and Sierra Leonean warring factions). In comparison to the first civil war in Liberia, the second Liberian war of 1999-2003 is even more rarely mentioned or assessed. By contrast, the sanctions against Charles Taylor's government, owing to his continued support of the RUF-rebels in Sierra Leone, and the deployment of the then highest number of UN-peacekeepers to a war-affected country following the signing of the Accra Agreement 2003, were indications for the increased international engagement in the Liberian conflict.

The scars of Liberia's civil wars are problems of the immediate present: about 13,000 peacekeepers of the United Nations Mission to Liberia (UNMIL) are still stationed in post-war Liberia, despite the inauguration of a democratically elected government in January 2006. This indicates that the government has not been able to guarantee the necessary security and satisfy the basic needs of the population without recourse to international aid. In spite of the fact that national reconstruction (especially in the hinterland) is far fetched from completion and there is only partially implemented reform process (most significantly in the security and rule of law sector[8]), it seems unlikely that a civil war will break out again. It is, therefore, the aim of this study to explain why the peace implementation phase I was not successful and violence erupted again, and why the peace implementation phases II and III were, to varying degrees, more successful in the stabilization of peace. Liberia was chosen as a single case study in order to conduct a more in-depth analysis of the civil war and to highlight the specific characteristics of the peace process. The research work is to offer explanations why numerous peace agreements and following implementation processes were required in order to end the conflict in Liberia.

The research questions can thus be enriched as follows: (1) *Which factors condition the success or failure of a peace process in the implementation phase of a new war?* (2) *Case-specific: Why did peace implementation fail in implementation phase I in comparison to implementation phases II and III?*

---

[8] See International Crisis Group 2006a, 2006b and 2009; Reports of the United Nations on the progress of UNMIL in Liberia (United Nations: Security Council, progress reports 2003-2007).

Definition of Peace

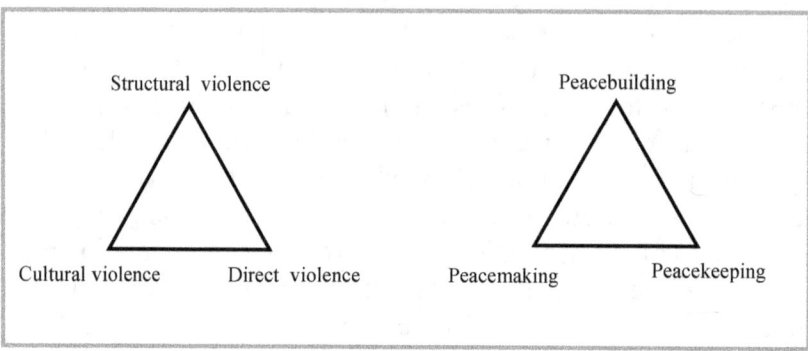

Figure 2.1 Galtung's models of violence and peace[9]

Peace cannot be separated from violence as Johan Galtung puts it, "to know about peace we have to know about violence".[10] The two concepts peace and violence are interlinked as the creation of peace "has to do with reducing violence (cure) and avoiding violence (prevention)".[11] Johan Galtung distinguishes between personal, direct and structural, indirect violence. If one considers peace as the absence of violence, then the broadening of the term violence also leads to a broadened peace term. That is, peace is then to be understood as the absence of personal and structural violence (as well as cultural violence in Galtung's later refinement of the concept – Figure 2.1). These two forms of peace (absence of personal and structural violence) are termed negative peace and positive peace respectively. Negative peace is the absence of hostilities or of the use of force; whether a legal state of war between the affected states and/or parties exists or not.[12] The mere termination of war or cessation of hostilities is generally already an enormous progress as even a bad state of

---

[9] Ramsbotham et al. 2005: 10.
[10] Galtung 1996: 9.
[11] ibid: 2.
[12] Woyke 2000: 250; cf. Ramsbotham et al. 2005: 10f.

8

peace is usually preferable to the state of war. It is, however, questionable if such a negative peace means stability. Beyond war termination, an agreement on a new order is necessary, which guarantees that politically significant conflicts in the future are carried out non-violently.[13] Positive peace goes beyond the absence of organised use of violence and is understood as a pattern of cooperation and integration of larger groups. The term includes, among others, the lack of exploitation, economic and social development, and the realization of human rights.[14] Thus, negative peace merely involves the cessation of personal, direct violence, while positive peace leads additionally to the overcoming of structural, indirect and cultural violence. All three components of violence, in turn, relate to the broader strategies of peacekeeping, peacebuilding and peacemaking (Figure 2.1).[15]

An evaluation of peace processes requires the deliberation on the understanding of peace: the presence of negative peace can easily be empirically determined. It is, however, more difficult to concretely determine a peace, which is more than non-war: does it mean the reduction or absence of indirect structural violence or the presence of social justice?[16] Is peace to be viewed from its temporal dimension (for example, peace equalling cease fire between two wars?); its content (peace equalling absence of direct, military as well as indirect, structural violence?); and/or its context (peace as a divisible, regional category, or only realized through world peace?)?[17] Herfried Münkler[18] questions whether the goal of positive peace can ever be achieved, as that, what man can be, is historically variable and can be itself a subject matter of violently carried out political controversies. It seems easier to use a practical, process-oriented peace term, which can be concretely substantiated and which gradually approaches the set requirements and targets. Dieter and Eva Senghaas[19] define peace as a demanding process of civilizing political collectives, the institutionalization of lasting, non-violent forms of conflict

---

[13] Krumwiede 1998: 38-40.
[14] Woyke 2000: 250.
[15] Ramsbotham et al. 2005: 10f.
[16] Matthies 1995: 27-29; Cf. Krumwiede 1998: 38-40.
[17] Woyke 2000: 243.
[18] Woyke 2000: 252.; Matthies 1995: 27-29; Krumwiede 1998: 38-40.
[19] ibid.

9

regulation. The supporting pillars of the blueprint of stable peace are a legitimate, effective monopoly of the use of force, rule of law, democratic participation, social justice, a control of affects, and a constructive conflict culture. The civilization hexagon model[20] helps to determine approximate values and to evaluate the stability of peace processes and peace consolidating measures. Peace can, thus, be determined in two different ways: peace as state or process.[21] Peace as "state" considers the mere regulation of conflicts as superficial and insufficient: one can only talk of peace when the cause of the conflict and the positional difference have been removed. Peace as "process" implies that the existence of social conflicts is inevitable and their resolution is extremely difficult and rare. Frank Schimmelpfennig[22] understands peace as a conflict practice based on process and solution, in the ideal case as a non-violent and fair process of conflict resolution; thus, combining the two forms of peace into one category. Peace is not only considered as the mere temporary absence of violence (for example, a limited cease fire) but as the lasting, institutionalized renouncement of its usage by the conflict parties. Conflict analysis[23], thus, has to be dynamic, that means, it has to include a diachronic, temporal dimension and has to consider changes over time. It has to encompass the development of the conflict, meaning the emergence of an incompatible positional difference, end with conflict resolution and record the change of all components of the conflict system within the overall time period.

Broad Concept of Peace Consolidation

Peace consolidation or "post-conflict peace-building", as termed in the *Agenda for Peace* report, is an "action to identify and support structures which will tend to strengthen and solidify peace in order to avoid a relapse into conflict."[24] The term "defines activities undertaken on the far side of conflict to

---

[20] ibid.
[21] Schimmelpfennig 1995: 30-32; Cf. Banks 1987.
[22] Schimmelpfennig 1995: 30-32.
[23] ibid.
[24] United Nations 1992: An Agenda for Peace, 21.

reassemble the foundations of peace and provide the tools for building on those foundations something that is more than just the absence of war."[25] Peace-building includes the reintegration of former combatants into civilian society, the strengthening of the rule of law; the improvement of respect for human rights through the monitoring, education and investigation of past and existing abuses; the provision of technical assistance for democratic development; and the promotion of conflict resolution and reconciliation techniques.[26]

Peace consolidation is to be located between war and peace as it is a state which is no longer war but not yet peace. A research project of the United Nations, therefore, talks of a conflict-to-peace continuum and of a peace/conflict environment, which has to be differentiated on a case-by-case basis.[27] Peace consolidation, according to Volker Matthies[28], is a complex, cross-social process of rehabilitation, reconstruction and renewal, which includes economical, social, psychological, humanitarian, political and security politics problem aspects, that have to be conceived and assessed as being in an overall integrative context. Moreover, the consolidation of peace is always already an element of prevention – that is, the prevention of a renewed outbreak of armed conflict. It results from the realization that peace is more than non-war and that such understood positive peace requires a target-oriented tackling of the underlying causes of armed conflicts as well as the rebuilding of a stable peace structure.[29] The United Nations, thus, endeavours to meet the new challenges through extended blue-helmet operations with civilian, humanitarian, political and development aid components, which go beyond traditional peacekeeping.[30]

Narrowing Down of Concept: Peace Implementation

Peace implementation is a narrowed down concept of peace consolidation. Peace consolidation, in comparison to peace

---

[25] United Nations 2000: Brahimi Report, 1:I.13.
[26] ibid.
[27] Matthies 1995: 22.
[28] ibid: 23.
[29] ibid: 18f.
[30] ibid: 19.

implementation, is a broad concept[31] as it encompasses the long-term stabilization and consolidation of peace in a war-affected country. Such cannot be achieved during the relative short phase of peace implementation. Peace implementation begins with the signing of the peace agreement and ends with the implementation of the peace agreement provisions:

> "Peace implementation is the process of carrying out a specific peace agreement. It focuses on the narrow, relatively short-term efforts (three months in the case of Zimbabwe, over five years in the case of Bosnia) to get warring parties to comply with their written commitments to peace"[32].

Peace implementation does not only have to include negative peace – the absence of war – but also to encompass elements of positive peace, such as, the overcoming of war consequences and the setting in of peace consolidating measures.[33] Barbara Walter[34] argues that the resolution of a civil war requires more than the mere institution of a cease fire: a successful peace settlement has to integrate previous warring factions into society, create a new government capable of accommodating their interests, and build a national, non-partisan military force. Peace implementation is, however, a very uncertain period as combatants are, in the face of demobilization and disarmament, less able to survive surprise attacks by other warring factions acting as spoilers. Thus, in the face of no or inadequate security guarantees by third parties, they might choose the safer option of war to peace; even if they signed a mutually agreed treaty beforehand.

Heinrich Krumwiede[35] advocates a strict differentiation between the implementation and consolidation phase; especially in order to find out which structural principles have priority in the implementation phase. The beginning of peace consolidation can, however, be difficult to demarcate as both phases can overlap: high-aiming goals like democratization, reconciliation and rule of law can be partly already noted in the peace agreement, and some mid- and long-term peace consolidating measures are already

---

[31] See United Nations 1992: Agenda for Peace, 21, 55, 57; United Nations 2000: Brahimi Report, 2-3:II.A.13.
[32] Stedman et al. 2002: 2.
[33] Cf. Matthies 1995: 11.
[34] Walter 2002: 6.
[35] Krumwiede 1998: 38-40.

instituted during the implementation phase. Peace implementing measures are, however, often a precondition before mid- and long-term peace consolidating measures can be instituted: the extent of the implementation of peace implementing measures is especially important in the security sector as a certain degree of security is necessary for the implementation of other measures.

The research work has as its central theme the transformation process from war to peace, with the focus on the transition phase between the signing of a peace agreement and the setting in of peace consolidation. Tasks of peace implementation are, for example, the demobilization, disarmament and reintegration of combatants, the instituting of reforms in the security sector and political institutions, the instituting of the reconstruction of the economy sector and infrastructure, and the preparation and execution of national elections. The next subchapter evaluates how other studies explain success or failure of war termination and which indicators have been found as determinant for success in the evaluated case studies. Chapter Three creates a theory model which specifically focuses on peace implementation and the factors which are determinant for its success or failure in the context of a new war.

Literature Overview of the Termination of Civil Wars

Explanatory Approaches and Success Factors for War Termination

In order to identify factors which can explain the success or failure of peace implementation, significant explanatory approaches and success factors for war termination in recent literature are presented in this subchapter.

Fen Osler Hampson[36] investigates why some peace agreements fail and others succeed in ending civil wars. Hampson proposes four success factors for his analysis of case studies: the extent of international nurturance of the peace process; the ripeness of the conflict as represented by the intrinsic

---

[36] Hampson 1996.

desire of the parties to make peace; systemic/regional power balances that favour peace; and the quality of the peace agreement itself (especially the inclusion of power-sharing arrangements). After application of the potential success factors on several internal conflicts, Hampson concludes that the outcome of a regulation fundamentally depends on the quality and the degree of the support provided by third parties to the peace process, especially during peace implementation. A regulation is, furthermore, positively influenced by a supportive regional and international environment.

Barbara Walter[37] explores the subject matter – why some combatants decide to sign and implement peace settlements, whilst others resume hostilities. Her study generates a theory of civil war settlement, which focuses on the problems combatants face during the credible commitment to the provisions of a peace agreement and their implementation. Walter argues that two specific factors ultimately determine whether groups sign and implement settlements or not: If security guarantees by third parties for the insecure demobilisation period and power-sharing guarantees in the first post-war government are pledged and provided to war factions, then the peace settlement will be implemented. If the warring factions do not get those guarantees, they will eventually reject the negotiated settlement and return to war.

Caroline Hartzell et al.[38] examine variables which can explain the longevity of negotiated peace settlements. On the basis of their analysis of 38 civil war settlements, they identify the context factors and settlement provisions which can affect the short-term stability of peace after a civil war. According to Hartzell et al., the results of their study show that many civil war contexts are more likely to lead to stable peace settlements than others: especially the offering of security guarantees and the inclusion of provisions of territorial autonomy in the peace settlements can increase the likelihood of a stable peace. It seems, furthermore, impossible to create lasting peace without explicitly solving the main issue of conflict.

---

[37] Walter 2002.
[38] Hartzell et al. 2001.

The investigation of the determinants of successful peace implementations in civil wars is the subject matter of Stephen John Stedman's study[39]. Stedman differentiates 16 conflicts in respect to the difficulty of their conflict environment and the degree of involvement of third parties in the implementation phase. According to Stedman, the two most significant conflict environment determinants for a failed peace implementation are the presence of spoilers (factions or leaders, which reject the peace agreement and use violence in order to undermine it) and neighbouring states, which reject the peace agreement and support spoilers. Furthermore, none of the analysed peace agreements was successfully implemented in countries where valuable, easily marketable natural resources like gemstones and timber are to be found. In countries with spoils, the implementing third parties should provide an appropriate strategy, corresponding resources and commitment to enable them to take action against the profiteers of war – peace implementation was only successful in the most difficult conflict environments when a major or regional power had a strategic interest in the conflict, was willing to provide resources and to risk troops.

Criticism

The presented explanatory approaches all underline the significance of a successful peace implementation for the peace process. According to Walter[40], the implementation phase is the most difficult phase to manage and the reason for the failure of many peace processes. The implementation phase is, however, not clearly defined. It is not or imprecisely differentiated from other terms such as peace consolidation or post-conflict peace building, or the time frame is too far-reaching. Stedman et al.[41], for example, define peace implementation as the implementation of a peace agreement: the operationalization of peace is, however, not based on the actual implementation of the peace agreement but on the possibility of the secure withdrawal of the

---

[39] Stedman 2001a, 2001b.
[40] Walter 2002: 4.
[41] Stedman et al. 2002: 2, 55ff.

implementing third party. Hartzell et al.[42] define peace as stability for five years. However, they exclude the degree of implementation of the peace agreement provisions from their definition. Hampson's definition of a successful settlement includes, alongside with the termination of hostilities, the establishment of institutions and supporting structures: peace implementation is not delimitated from peace consolidation.

The peace agreement implementation is fundamentally the implementation of the stipulated sub-goals within the agreement. Stedman differentiates between the most important and less important sub-goals for the implementation phase: the demobilisation of combatants and demilitarisation of politics are to be given priority. According to Stedman[43], civil wars cannot be terminated without the attainment of these two sub-goals and other goals such as the consolidation of democracy and the protection of human rights have then only a limited chance of succeeding. Walter, Hampson and Hartzell et al. all emphasize the importance of guarantees (power-sharing/security guarantees) provided by third parties and restrict the role of third parties to such provision rather than investigating their input into the implementation of other sub-goals and/or considering the priority of certain sub-goals over others.

The selected civil wars are mostly presented in an undifferentiating manner: civil wars can, for example, differ with respect to the nature of their conflict and the motives of the war actors. This has consequences for the degree of required international commitment for the conflict settlement and the overall peace process. Hampson does not include in his analysis, how many resources have to be committed to a specific conflict, in order to attain a successful settlement. Walter does not consider in regard to the degree of international commitment that wars differ due to their nature of conflict. As such, each conflict provides specific, unique challenges for implementing third parties, which is only comparable to a different conflict to a certain extent.

---

[42] Hartzell et al. 2001: 2, 9-10.
[43] Stedman 2001b: 3.

Hampson chooses as one of the factors, which affects the success prospects of a settlement, the design of the peace agreement. The cited indicators[44] are, however, too broadly conceptualized and not precisely amplified (ambiguity, bad design). Thus, some aspects of the conditions design of the peace agreement, conflict nature and degree of international commitment are included in the explanatory approaches but they are not set in a common context and the relations between them are not established – to what extent a certain factor and its negative or positive characteristics have an effect on the peculiarities of another factor.

All four presented explanatory approaches do not investigate the decision processes of conflict parties and the conditions, which influence their preferences and expectations and therefore their behaviour. One of Stedman's determinants of the conflict environment is the presence of spoilers[45]: spoiler-benefiting structures are, however, not related to the actor, and the decision process of the spoiler and the consequences of this decision process are not elaborated on. Hampson und Hartzell et al. do not consider the actor's level: they restrict their analysis to the role of third parties and their provision of guarantees to the conflict parties.

The insufficient consideration of the structure and actor level and their relation to each other are also to be seen in regard to the changes in warfare: the change from old to new wars is particularly marked by the increasing privatisation and denationalisation of organised, collective use of force. New wars entail a high risk of the perpetuation of violence, and peace settlements remain fragile in many countries with failing or failed state structures. As a consequence of the changes in warfare, the context factors of the new wars and the required strategies and measures in settling a new war have to be incorporated in the explanatory approach, so that a successful or failed peace implementation can be explained in such a context. The interests and expectations of the war actors have, furthermore, to be judged in the context of changed structures and conditions. The

---

[44] Hampson 1996: 3-4.
[45] Stedman 2001b: 2, 12.

hitherto explanatory approaches cannot sufficiently explain new wars and their settlement due to their non-consideration of the change in warfare on the structure and actor level (except some aspects in Stedman's works) or they rather cannot depict the overall picture of a new war. The following subchapter presents the concept of new wars in detail.

Concept of New Wars

Definition of War

War is generally regarded as an armed conflict between two parties (with at least one of the parties being the government of a state), which crosses the threshold of at least 1000 battle-related deaths. In order to exclude one-sided attacks, massacres or sporadic violence, casualties are to be ascertained on both sides. It is, furthermore, characteristic of war that the hostilities bear a certain continuity and follow an overall strategy, and that the warring factions are at least partly centrally organised[46]. The Uppsala Conflict Data Program adds a further criterion in their definition of an armed conflict – the requirement that the conflict is to have a "contested incompatibility" as its basis.[47]

Civil wars are a specific manifestation of the general phenomenon war[48] and are basically characterized by their particular doggedness and cruelty[49], in which civilians fight against civilians within the same state: the physical nearness of combatants marks the particular cruelness of civil wars. Waldmann[50] argues that in the context of states with weak political structures, civil wars remove themselves from the model character of interstate wars and can lead to the collapse of such states. According to van Creveld[51], 'low intensity wars' do not only modify the state-centred model of war but also

---

[46] Cf. Uppsala Conflict Data Program 2006b; Hofmeier/Mehler 2004: 163; Waldmann 1998: 15; Imbusch/Zoll 2006: 114-115; Woyke 2000.
[47] Uppsala Conflict Data Program 2006b.
[48] Waldmann 1998: 15.
[49] ibid: 18.
[50] ibid: 15ff.
[51] Cf. Waldmann 1998: 22-26; van Creveld 1991: 20-22, 192-195, 200-221.

fundamentally question it: firstly, they are no longer only fought for the contest of state power but can also be an end in itself; secondly, they rarely involve regular armed forces on both sides and the dividing line between combatants and civilians is increasingly disappearing, which implies that the separation of government, army and civilian is unstoppable, and the state will lose the monopoly on the use of force to a different kind of organisation; and, thirdly, the internationally recognized norms of warfare are no longer effective because of the increasing deregulation of civil wars and the change in the war motivation of combatants. Waldmann notes that the degree of the consideration of rules decreases from the interstate to the internal war: a disappearing commitment to rules can be observed in warfare in ethical-moral as well as technical respects.[52] Georg Elwert even goes as far as calling modern war zones 'gewaltoffene Räume' – war zones that are characterized by the absence of a monopoly on the use of force and where no fixed rules limit the use of force (by armed forces of the state and/or private actors).[53]

A war can be defined on the basis of the participating actors, the duration of the hostilities and the intensity of the violence and can, thereby, be distinguished from non-warring violence, on the one hand, and from other wars through the specificities of the three factors, on the other hand.[54] Wars can, furthermore, be typologised in different ways: they can be distinguished with respect to their war type, or the change of warfare itself can be the object of differentiation. Chojnacki[55] introduces a typologisation of war, which attempts to differentiate wars on the basis of the socialisation type or the political status of the actors. Four types of warlike violence result out of this classification: interstate wars; extra-state wars; internal wars; and sub-state wars. Chojnacki differentiates between war types on different levels, on the one hand, and considers the change in warfare, on the other hand. The fourth war type – sub-state war – can be delimited from internal war by the change in actors and, thereby, mirrors the change in warfare on the internal level: the

---

[52] Waldmann 1998: 26f.
[53] ibid: 28f.
[54] Imbusch/Zoll 2006: 109-111.
[55] Chojnacki 2006; 2008a, b.

operationalization and delimitation to internal wars considers that, first of all, private actors of violence dominate in areas of failing or failed statehood; and, secondly, the criterion of 1,000 killed soldiers has to be extended to include civilian victims of direct military violence, due to the disappearing division between combatants and civilians. Figure 2.2 exemplifies the dominance of intra-state wars at the global level since World War II and a significant increment of sub-state wars over the last two decades.[56]

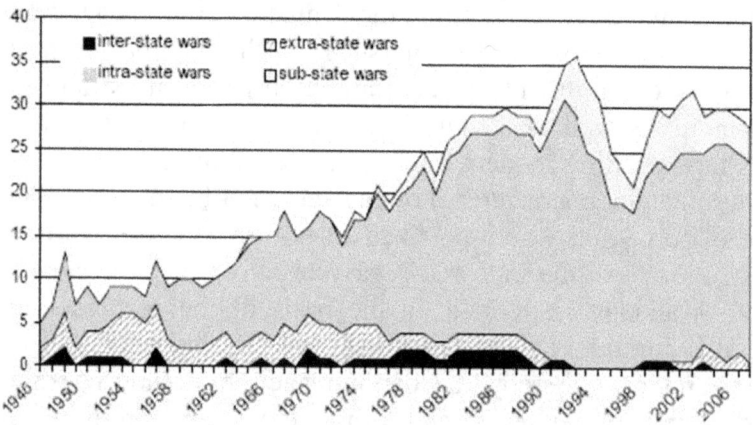

Figure 2.2   Ongoing wars by type, 1946-2007[57]

Features of New Wars

The concept of "new wars" describes a change in warfare and distinguishes between "old" and "new" wars. Mary Kaldor[58] introduced the term "new" war in order to differentiate between the classical interstate wars and the new wars. Although most of new wars occur locally, they have diverse transnational linkages so that the heretofore clear distinctions between internal and external, local and global can no longer be maintained.[59] They have to be conceived within the context of intensified global linkages, which are, for example, reflected in the presence of

---

[56] Chojnacki 2008b: 235.
[57] ibid.
[58] Kaldor 1999.
[59] ibid: 2-3.

mercenaries as well as non-governmental organisations in war zones.

Herfried Münkler takes up the distinction between old and new wars and, in comparison to Kaldor, puts more emphasis on the transition from interstate to new, denationalized wars.[60] Due to the complexity of the causes of conflict and motives of violence[61], Münkler uses the term "new war" to encompass the change in warfare. He, however, qualifies the New character of contemporary wars as aspects of the new war type can be found in older forms of warfare: the melange of diverse interests and values of actors during the Thirty Years' War resembles the variety of violence motives in the new war model. The comparison with older war types serves to highlight the features and particularities of the new wars.

According to Münkler[62], new wars do not emerge, like the old wars, from state-building process but from state-failing or denationalization processes. New wars take place in environments which are marked by the subversion of the state's monopoly on the use of force: firstly, by the transnationalisation of military armed forces, and, secondly, by the privatisation of violence.[63] States are replaced as the main actors of war by para-state, partly private actors – local warlords, mercenary firms. Many of them are war entrepreneurs, which wage war on their own account and procure their needed assets through different ways and means.[64] The privatisation of violence became particularly possible because warfare in the new wars is relatively cheap with regard to the use of light weapons and the therewith-linked deployment of child soldiers.[65]

The financing of war is, in comparison to the classic state wars, an important aspect of warfare itself. The various factions finance their war activities through the transfer of assets – robbery, looting, 'war taxes', the sale of drilling and mining rights -, the trade in drugs, natural resources and arms, and external assistance – direct assistance from the diaspora, financial

---

[60] Imbusch/Zoll 2006: 111-113.
[61] Münkler 2002: 9.
[62] ibid: 10, 36-40.
[63] ibid: 2-6.
[64] ibid: 7.
[65] ibid: 10, 36-40.

or other support by other states and diversion of humanitarian aid.[66] The changed forms of finance also contribute to the longer duration of new wars because economic interests are inextricably linked with them.[67] The war legitimizes diverse criminal forms of private enrichment whilst those are at the same time necessary financial sources for the perpetuity of war.

The warring parties need more or less permanent conflict in order to reproduce their power positions and for the access to resources. Whilst those predatory social relations are the most pronounced in the war zones, they also characterize the surrounding regions. Neighbouring states are those which are immediately affected: reduced trade, influx of refugees, proliferation of illegal trade and the infringing of identity politics are factors which reproduce the conditions of the war zones and nurture new forms of violence.[68] Chojnacki[69] details the danger of the emergence of complex regional conflict systems and transnational orders of violence in areas of limited or failed statehood: they are either caused by strategic and economic interests of neighbouring states and non-state groups, that are willing to resort to violence, (DR Congo, for example) or by the operations of warlords like Charles Taylor in Liberia, which do not only influence the local environment but also the conflict dynamics in the neighbouring states. Warfare often shifts from the political control of the capital to the politico-economical control of strategically important natural resources and trade routes.

The autonomization of warlike violence is a particularity of the new wars in which unequal opponents fight against each other. There are rarely battles between the warring factions: the violence is for the most part directed against the civilian population and tends to be lacking all constraints.[70] The civilian population is intimidated by excessive violence and subjected to the will of the combatants by means of the stoking of fears. New warfare borrows the strategy of controlling areas by political

---

[66] Cf. Kaldor 1999: 107-111.
[67] Münkler 2002: 10, 36-40.
[68] Kaldor 1999: 107-111.
[69] Chojnacki 2006: 62.
[70] Imbusch/Zoll 2006: 111-113

control rather than capturing areas of opposing troops from guerrilla warfare. Ideology was important to the revolutionaries: even when fear was an important element, the central goal was the support and loyalty to the revolutionary idea. The new warriors, by contrast, establish political control through loyalty to their group than to an idea. The control on their side does not depend on positive allotments but on continuous fear and insecurity and the fuelling of hate towards others. What were considered undesirable and illegitimate side effects of old wars are now central to the warfare of new wars. [71] Even if small groups are not satisfied with the conditions, which become apparent as characterizing the state of peace, it is an easy task for them to rekindle the war.[72] Peace processes are, therefore, only successful when third parties mediate between the warring factions. However, it is essential for the mediating party to have the required resources needed to suppress the elements of violence and institute peace attractive to the warring parties.[73]

Criticism or Relevance of Concept

Critics[74] of the concept of new wars note that the new wars are not new phenomena and their features can already be observed before the end of the Cold War. They criticise the overemphasis of the newness of the so-called new war type. The theoretical concept is, secondly, not sufficiently precise as general processes are described, and the term "new war" is left too broad as it also encompasses, for example, phenomena like terrorism. Thirdly, Kaldor applies the concept to only one case study (Bosnia): critics raise the issue whether the concept can only be applied to this case or similar cases, or whether it can also explain cases from other world regions.[75]

'Slow' changes in warfare as well as the consequential challenges, arising for the termination of war, are also discerned

---

[71] Kaldor 1999: 101.
[72] Münkler 2002: 27-28.
[73] ibid: 28.
[74] Cf. Berdal 2003; Chojnacki 2004; Matthies 2004; Schlichte 2006.
[75] Except Heupel/Zangl 2004; Heupel 2005: Heupel and Zangl apply the concept to several cases of diverse world regions.

by critics of the concept. Chojnacki[76] notes that it was important to describe new trends and changes in contemporary warfare and to question, whether these observed changes require new theoretical explanations; the 'newness' is, however, not to be overrated. According to Chojnacki, the autonomy and political status of actors of violence has changed in denationalised areas, as well as their conflict-theoretical significance.[77] Despite eligible criticism of the concept, argues Matthies, it is ultimately not about whether the controversially discussed features and combinations of features are actually NEW or not but HOW they are. Only knowledge of contemporary conflicts of violence, which is in line with reality, enables the conceptualization of appropriate security and peace promoting counter-strategies.[78]

Implications of New Wars Features on Peace Implementation

The features of the new wars – especially the motives of the war actors, the type of warfare and the financing of war activities – have consequences for the success prospects of peace implementation. First of all, they determine the level of difficulty of the conflict environment, and, secondly, their associated consequences on the management of the conflict follow that the latter has to be attuned to the characteristics of the conflict. On this account, the characteristics of new wars have to be included in the formulation of the factors, which explain success or failure of peace implementation. The key factor for successful peace consolidation in new wars is, according to Monika Heupel[79], the consideration of the change in form of economies of violence. For example, several peace agreements could not be implemented in the first half of the 1990s Liberian civil war because, among other things, influential warlords profited from the trade with natural resources and could thereby (re)arm their combat units.[80]

Heupel presents the design of 'traditional' peaceconsolidating measures as an alternative explanatory factor.

---

[76] Chojnacki 2004: 17.
[77] ibid: 17.
[78] Matthies 2004: 4.
[79] Heupel 2005.
[80] ibid: 17.

Success or failure of peace consolidation can also depend on how high or low the quality of the design of 'traditional' peaceconsolidating measures is. The integration of all relevant conflict parties in the first post-conflict government could, for example, be beneficial for the success prospects of peace consolidation. Heupel, however, qualifies the role of 'traditional' peaceconsolidating measures as the strategies for the weakening of criminalised economies of violence are an important precondition for the implementation of 'traditional' measures.

Her focus is, therefore, on the implementation of effective strategies for the weakening of criminalised economies of violence, which are to restrict the financing options of spoilers for their war activities. In most cases, strategies for the weakening of criminalised economies of violence are, however, implemented simultaneously with other measures in the implementation phase like, for example, reform of institutions. As postulated by Heupel, the strategies for the weakening of criminalised economies of violence are thus not necessarily preconditions for other measures. An exception is, for example, the sanctions against the Taylor government, which were effected by the UN-Security Council before the signing of the peace agreement in 2003. The sanctions still had an effect on the peace implementation after 2003 as they were lifted during the term of office of the first democratically elected post-war government.

Strategies for the weakening of criminalised economies of violence cannot explain the success or failure of peace implementation on their own: other factors like context factors (for example, state failure), degree of international commitment[81], design of the peace agreement[82] and nature of conflict (for example, the number of warring factions) have to be factored in to present the overall picture of peace implementation in a new war and to be able to explain its success or failure. A theory model is generated in the following chapter, which attempts to consider the above mentioned factors.

---

[81] The role of third parties is, in Heupel's study, only considered as an indicator of peaceconsolidating measures.
[82] Peaceconsolidating measures are only judged with respect to their implementation: Heupel does not investigate whether the design of the peace agreement itself was deficient and thus affected the implementation of the measures.

It is to be assessed in the analysis of the case study on Liberia how far the peculiarities of new wars played a role in the settlement of the conflict, and to what extent they were considered in the formulation of the peace agreement and during the implementation of the peaceimplementing strategies. It is especially of interest if and to what extent the strategies differ in the three peace implementation phases.

THREE

Theoretical and Methodical Specifications

Derivation of Theoretical Model and Research Hypotheses

Rational Choice Theory

Rational choice theory is a multidisciplinary explanatory approach – employed in economics, sociology and political science - which proceeds on the assumption of rational actions: patterns of behaviour in society reflect the choices made by individuals as they try to maximize their benefits and minimize their costs.[83] The rational choice approach, according to Volker Kunz[84], can be summed up in five statements. First, the individual is the unit of action: methodological individualism assumes that all social phenomena are considered as the result of aggregated attitudes, decisions and actions of individuals. Secondly, the actions of individuals follow self-interest: individual decisions and actions, which underlie collective phenomena, are based on rational contemplations, which conform to the principle of utility maximization. It means that the actors attempt to realize their needs, goals, wishes or preferences to the highest possible extent. The well-being of others is not excluded from the general definition of self interest: it is, however, dependent on the utility a person assigns to it. Thirdly, scarcity determines human living conditions as actors have to evaluate

---

[83] Wikipedia: Rational Choice Theory, 2.
[84] Kunz 2004: 10-12.

preferable alternatives in dependence of given restrictions. Actors have to choose among preferred alternatives the action which provides the highest benefit and the lowest cost in attaining their goal(s). As one abdicates, in the execution of action A, the utility, which one could achieve through an alternative action B, one speaks in this context of alternative or opportunity costs of action. They are defined as the foregone utility of the next best, not chosen, alternative action. Fourth, human nature is constant and transcends cultures, periods and societies: every actor acts in a certain way, which promises the highest degree of goal achievement in respect to his or her convictions about the 'state of the world'. And fifth, social processes and structures are the unplanned result of deliberate individual actions: individual motives of action and collective consequences of action do not have to conform (and frequently do not). Future actions in turn result from the collective consequences of action.

Rational choice entails general assumptions on the kind and manner of how collective phenomena are to be assessed. These assumptions are based on the idea of a reciprocal linkage of social structures and individual choices of action. Social phenomena result from individual decisions and actions, and these choices of action are always embedded in social structures. This means, collective phenomena are the framing conditions as well as the result of individual courses of action. This approach is called structure individualistic. A characteristic of this approach is the proceeding in three steps: the logic of situation establishes the relation between social situation and actor; the logic of selection explains the individual course of action; and the logic of aggregation links the individual actions with the actual collective, social facts of interest.[85] The collective explananda at the macro level are at the centre of the analysis as they essentially explain the social phenomena that are of interest; however, collective phenomena are always the result of individual actions at the micro level. The single actors, in turn, are embedded in social contexts, which provide conditions for their actions (opportunities and constraints). The extent to which the actor's goals can be realized, depends on the action restrictions or

---

[85] Kunz 2004: 12-25.

opportunities in a certain situation, which have to be specified in the analysis of a specific case. In every concrete case of application, the ancillary conditions have to be newly determined because they cannot be deductively derived from the theory of rational choice. The structure individualistic perspective focuses in this context on the formulation and empirical filling of bridging assumptions, which link the variables of the level of action with social reality. The empirical filling of the action theoretical construct leads to an analysis of the social situation of interest.[86] The theoretical model of Figure 3.1 considers the basic assumptions of the theory of rational choice – with regards to the rational, deliberate and utility-maximizing acting of individual actors – and bases its structural differentiation between a macro and micro level and the cyclical linkage and interdependence of structural and individual levels on the structure individualistic approach.

Theoretical Model

The preceding chapters demonstrated that the established explanatory approaches could not sufficiently explain the new type of war. The concept of new wars is, furthermore, as yet too abstract: for example, the interrelations between structure and actors are not sufficiently explicated and not brought into a clear order so that the action process can be traced and the resulting consequences for the progress of a peace process can be identified. A theory model peace implementation in a new war (Figure 3.1) is generated in this chapter, taking the inadequacies of the established approaches and concepts as a challenge to be overcome. The model derives from the rational choice model the basic assumptions on the interactions between structure and agency, macro and micro level. The research work amplifies that both structure and agency have to be assessed in the peace implementation of a new war in order to depict the causal process from independent to dependent variable adequately and, specifically, to highlight the interplay between structural

---

[86] Kunz 2004: 41.

conditions and the decisions of actors to cooperate or not in peace implementation.

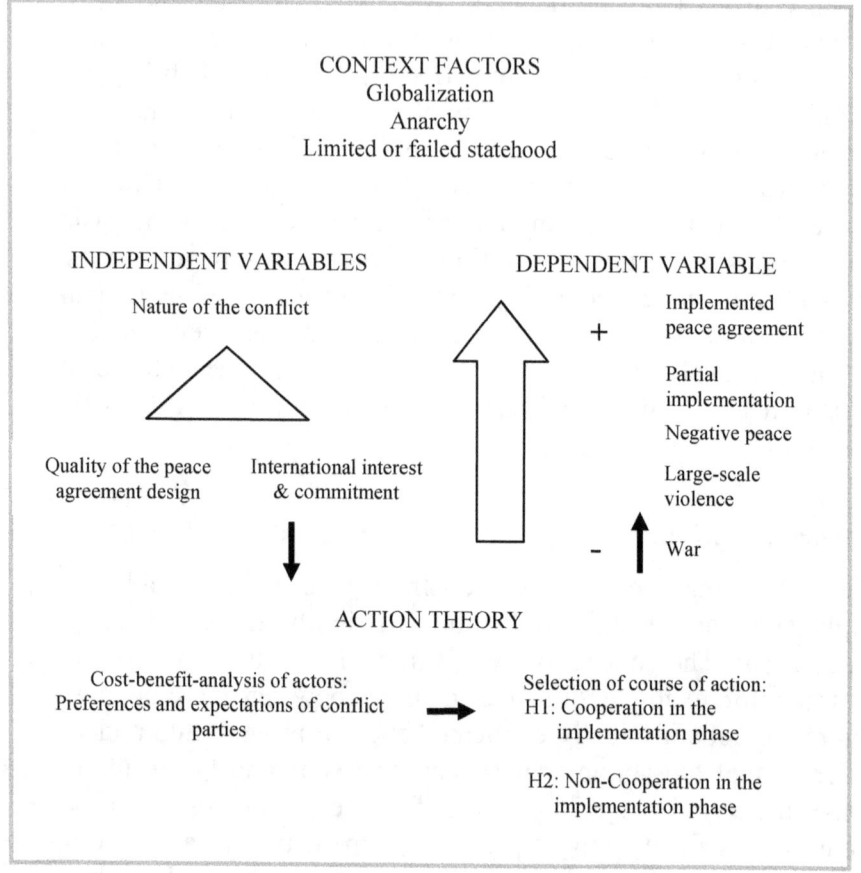

Figure 3.1   Theory model – peace implementation in a new war

The context factors and conditions, which have an influence on the behaviour of the actors and the structuring of the war or the peace process, are taken as the point of departure. The actions of the actors are, due to these conditions, subject to constraints and opportunities. Against this background, the actors select the course of action which appears to be the most beneficial for the achievement of their goals at the particular point in time. The aggregation of the individual selection processes has, in turn, impacts on the macro level – success or failure of peace implementation. The individual steps of the model are further detailed in the subsequent subchapters.

Context Factors

Anarchy

The international system is composed of units – sovereign states – which do not recognize a power superior to them.[87] "No international legislature makes laws to regulate the relations between states", argues James C. Roberts. "And no supreme executive stands ready to inhibit the actions of a single state when those actions oppose the common will."[88] Due to this absence of a supranational governing body, the international system is described as an anarchical system, which means that no supra-state keeps order as a supreme law-maker or law-enforcer and guarantees the security of the states and the adherence to agreed-upon rules.[89] Anarchy is thus defined as the absence of a supranational monopoly on the use of force.[90]

The anarchical structure of the international system creates a security dilemma for the sovereign states: they are reliant on self-help in order to guarantee their survival and independence under the condition of anarchy. According to neo-realism, the more power they possess in comparison to other states, the higher is their ability for self-help and the higher is their security and independence in the international system.[91] From this results that "wars occur because there is nothing to stop [the states] when a state believes it must defend or further a "vital interest" by force"[92]. According to rational institutionalism, international politics can no longer be appropriately described as a natural state or war of all against all: the interdependence problems of the present can only be managed through cooperation. Even under the condition of anarchy, states are able to establish and sustain international institutions which manage

---

[87] Rittberger 2001a.
[88] Roberts: 1.
[89] Cf. Rittberger 2001; Roberts; Linklater 2000.
[90] Rittberger 2003: 35.
[91] Rittberger 2001a.
[92] Linklater 2000: 327.

their common problems in the absence of a supra-state government.[93] Order in the international system is, thus, the result more of cooperation than of a conflictual standoff of a balance-of-power (in comparison to neo-realism).[94]

Furthermore, anarchy is not "synonymous with disorder or chaos. There is no a priori reason to conclude that the emergence of effective systems of rights and rules is infeasible in polities characterized by a high degree of decentralization with respect to the distribution of authority and power"[95]. "States", notes Linklater, "form a primitive society, with rules, norms and values (such as international law, diplomacy and sovereignty)", which "cushions states from each other"[96]. Such societal element of the interstate system led Hedley Bull to describe it as "the anarchical society"[97]. Through the promotion of human rights and the transfer of resources, according to Bull, states in the UN are committed to more than the preservation of their security interests.[98] Linklater argues, however, that "it is necessary to go beyond Bull's "anarchical society" of states to an anarchical global "community of communities"" [99] in order to achieve security under the condition of anarchy: the concern is to create "positive relationships based not only on reciprocal obligations and mutual self-interest (*Gesellschaft*) but also on a sense of loyalty and moral obligation (*Gemeinschaft*)"[100]. Linklater thus understands anarchy not as "the essence of the problem to be overcome" but as "the framework for thinking about the *solution* to global problems"[101]. Anarchy is, therefore, the context in which global problems occur but is not considered as the fundamental issue at hand.

---

[93] Rittberger 2001b.
[94] Roberts: 2.
[95] Young 1978: 272; cited in: Roberts: 1.
[96] Linklater 2000: 324.
[97] ibid: 324.
[98] Bull; cited in: Linklater 2000: 333.
[99] Linklater 2000: 333.
[100] ibid: 333.
[101] ibid: 333.

Globalization

Globalization describes intensified global social relations between people, which reside at different locations and are disengaged from time and space restrictions: according to Scholte, globalization is, thus, "the spread of transplanetary – and in recent times also more particularly supraterritorial – connections between people"[102]. The spatial dimension of globalization is also taken up by Held et al.: globalization is generally considered as "the widening, deepening and speeding up of worldwide interconnectedness in all aspects of contemporary social life, from the cultural to the criminal, the financial to the spiritual" [103]. Beyond the acknowledgement of the intensification of global interconnectedness, there is disagreement between the representatives of the schools of thought as to how globalization is to be conceptualized. Held et al. distinguish between three broad schools of thought: the hyperglobalizers, the sceptics and the transformationalists.

For the hyperglobalizers, contemporary globalization is foremost an economic phenomenon: "economic globalization is bringing about a 'denationalization' of economies through the establishment of transnational networks of production, trade and finance"[104]. It affects the authority and legitimacy of the traditional nation states to control what occurs within their own borders or to satisfy the needs of their own citizens: states and their citizens are increasingly subjected to regional and global mechanisms of governance. Nation states are "increasingly becoming 'a transitional mode of organization for managing economic affairs'"[105] than holding sole economic and political power within their states. The rise of the global economy, the emergence of institutions of regional and global governance, and the global diffusion and hybridization of cultures are signs of a new world order, preconfiguring the regressiveness of statehood.[106]

---

[102] Scholte 2005: 59.
[103] Held et al. 1999: 2.
[104] ibid: 3.
[105] ibid: 5.
[106] ibid: 3-5.

The sceptics argue that globalization "implies a perfectly integrated worldwide economy in which the 'law of one price' prevails"[107]. However, contemporary levels of economic interdependence are, according to the sceptics, only characterized by "heightened levels of internationalization, that is, interactions between predominantly national economies"[108]. The extent of contemporary globalization is, thus, in comparison to economic integration levels of the 19th century, exaggerated, and that processes of internationalization fundamentally depend on the regulatory power of national governments. A current regionalization of economic activity can rather be perceived – a development of three major financial and trading blocs - which constitutes an opposing trend to globalization: the international economy has become "less global in its geographical embrace"[109] in comparison with the world empires of the 19th century. Contrary to the hyperglobalists' notion of a global culture, the sceptics hold that the world is fragmented into civilizational blocs, and cultural and ethnic enclaves due to the deeply rooted patterns of inequality and hierarchy in the world economy.[110]

Transformationalists do not "evaluate the present in relation to some single, fixed ideal-type 'globalized world'"[111], such as a global market or global civilization, nor do they make claims about the future development of globalization. Globalization is conceived as a dynamic and open-ended historical process, characterized by contradicting tendencies. Contemporary globalization, nonetheless, stands out due to the historically unprecedented "patterns of global economic, military, technological, ecological, migratory, political and cultural flows"[112]. It is not, however, understood as a state of global convergence as new patterns of global stratification lead, on the one hand, to the increasing involvement of some states, societies and communities in the global order and, on the other hand, the increasing marginalization of others. According to transformationalists, states no longer retain sole command over

---

[107] Held et al. 1999: 5.
[108] ibid.
[109] ibid.
[110] ibid: 5-7.
[111] ibid: 7.
[112] ibid.

what transpires within their own territories due to the expanding jurisdiction of institutions of regional and/or global governance. The changing global order, however, encourages coherent adjustment strategies of states in order to adapt to "the growing complexity of processes of governance in a more interconnected world"[113]. Complex global systems connect communities of different regions of the world in different areas such that many aspects of contemporary economic and social life are today transnationally rather than nationally organized. Globalization is thus associated with a transformation of the relationship between sovereignty, territoriality and state power.[114]

According to Held et al.[115], globalization is best conceived as a process or a set of processes rather than a singular condition, such as a world community. The global processes are considered as a differentiated and multifaceted process: firstly, the overlapping and interacting networks of global interconnectedness impose constraints on as well as empower communities and states; secondly, they have an impact on all social domains (cultural, economic, political, military, etc.); and thirdly, socio-economic and political space is best described as aterritorial as it has deterritorial as well as reterritorial tendencies. Furthermore, the sites and exercise of power become increasingly distant from the subjects experiencing their impact. Globalization is thus more specifically defined as a transformational process of the spatial organization of social relations and transactions in regard to their extensity, intensity, velocity and impact. This transformation process generates transcontinental and interregional exchange processes, and networks of activity, interaction and the exercise of power across vast distances.[116]

Global and regional processes and the changed constitution of state authority have to be considered in the analysis of new, intra-state wars in order to capture their complexity and global and regional interconnectedness: according to Jung, "the causes and impacts of new wars are neither confined to a single zone of

---

[113] Held et al. 1999: 9.
[114] ibid: 7-9.
[115] ibid: 27f.
[116] ibid: 16.

conflict, nor are they limited by the territorial demarcation lines of war-torn states."[117] Structures of violence at the local level are, therefore, essentially connected to the global economy and international power relations.[118]

Contemporary globalization is accompanied by the emergence of violent war economies in war-affected regions: warring parties forge collaborations with international corporations, criminal networks and/or states to trade illegally acquired goods for the financing of their war activities. "[T]he marketing of local resources and procurement of arms and supplies", argues Duffield, "are based on access to global markets and, very often, transcontinental smuggling or gray commercial networks."[119] The warring factions are, thus, reliant on external linkages for their economic sustainability. Furthermore, the "[w]ar entrepreneurs in the zone of conflict are at the same time local, national and global economic players, investing their financial assets in the zone of peace"[120], causing the distinctions between formal and shadow economies to be blurred.

New, intra-state wars are, on the other hand, affected by local, regional and international policies of peacemaking, peace enforcement and peace implementation: different actors at multiple levels of governance contribute to the peace process and, in particular, the regulation of the war economy, for example, by the offering or threatening of incentives such as guarantees or sanctions. "Given the dependence of war economies on international trade networks", argues Duffield, "[the warring parties] are vulnerable to a concerted application of appropriate compliance and regulatory measures."[121] Reducing the profitability and effectiveness of conflict-related transborder trade networks is, however, to be complemented by other measures, such as confidence-building and political reform measures, in order to lead to a consolidated peace.[122]

---

[117] Jung 2003: 5.
[118] ibid: 2.
[119] Duffield 2000: 75.
[120] Jung 2003: 3.
[121] Duffield 2000: 85.
[122] ibid: 85.

Failing or Failed State

The actual historical background to the discussion on fragile or failed states is that liberal hopes were not fulfilled, which held that the opening of the markets and the holding of elections would lead to the pacification of social conflicts in every political context. On the contrary, since the 1980s foreign economic opening, reduction of the state apparatus and democratic competition go alongside with loss of wealth and political violence. The concept "state failure" was thus, according to Klaus Schlichte[123], coined to fill the gap created by the empirical failure of the liberalist model, considering the perils of peripheral statehood such as its destabilizing effect on international order in general and its connection to the emergence of new wars and transnational terrorism more specifically. State failure is in two respects conceived as a problem: first, as a security problem, and, secondly, as a profound hindrance of development. Authors on the security political side of state failure do not only focus on classical security issues but also link them to humanitarian concerns, for example, the inefficiency of corruption, the plight of war victims and the activities of organised crime like trade in drugs and human trafficking. Global terrorism, new wars and organised crime are particularly prominent in these deliberations on state failure. Afghanistan is cited as an example for security political threats because international terrorism relies on such fragile states in order to reproduce itself.[124] From a development political perspective, the underperformance in central state functions consists in the inability of states to shield their citizens from violence, the deficient control of power, the sole functioning of state services and tax collection in the cities, the absence of reliable basic conditions for the economy and the rudimentary provision of social care. This has caused donors to shun such states, concentrating on so-called "good performers".[125]

State failure is understood as the inability of the state apparatus to execute sovereign tasks, to provide 'political goods' like security, education, health services and economic

---

[123] Schlichte 2008: 136f.
[124] ibid: 140f.
[125] Debiel 2005: 12, cited in: Schlichte 2008: 141.

opportunities for development, a legal basis for public order as well as a justice system to administrate them, and finally fundamental infrastructural conditions like streets and opportunities of communication.[126] The state is especially affected by its swindling ability to regulate technologies, capital flows, ecological processes and actions of transnational corporations on the national state level.[127] According to I. William Zartman, a state is "the authoritative political institution that is sovereign over a recognized territory", which fundamentally has three functions: "the state as the sovereign authority – the accepted source of identity and the arena of politics; the state as an institution – and therefore a tangible organization of decision-making and an intangible symbol of identity; and the state as the security guarantor for a populated territory."[128] A weakening of one function affects the effectiveness of the other state's functions. Thus, state collapse means that the state no longer performs its basic functions, in terms of a decision-making, executing and enforcing institution, and the like. State collapse is, however, not a short-term process: I. William Zartman likens the state failing process to the progress of an object tumbling down a staircase, landing and teetering on each step it hits, either regaining its balance or bouncing down to the next step. Many states recover from their downward fall and return to more or less normal functions: only the states that reach the bottom of the stairs can be called collapsed. Thus, states can be at different stages of the downward 'failing' spiral – failing, failed or collapsed – depending on the extent of their loss of state authority and ability to exercise state functions.

The states' elements are fundamentally affected under the condition of global processes: firstly, a state's territory is relativized by fragmentation processes from within and by the emergence of major economic areas and political integration as well as by technological developments, and permeable borders from without; secondly, a state's populace becomes more heterogeneous due to the increment of worldwide migration movements; and, thirdly, the effective use of a state's authority is

---

[126] Ruf 2003: 24.
[127] ibid: 10.
[128] Zartman 1995: 5.

hampered by the transformation of the state's organisation structures and control mechanisms due to the processes of delegation, deregulation, and decentralization.[129] States are no longer able to fulfil their traditionally assigned tasks, which in turn affects their legitimacy in the eyes of their populace. Joachim Hirsch[130] argues that the development of the state to a negotiating rather than an acting state, the increased importance of informal international networks, the transfer of processes of consent building and decision-making to the regional as well as the international level and the restriction of economic- and socio-political intervention capacities of the states due to globalization encompass a significant weakening of single-state democratic systems and generate a structural deficit of legitimacy.

State failure is often considered less from its economical and social causes but as an accompaniment of violently carried out conflict. It is argued that in former socialist countries, present intra-state conflicts reappear at the surface after the breakdown of the central exercise of power. Other works conceive the cause of state failure to be due to the role of external powers or their decreasing interest because of the strategic loss of importance of these states after the end of bipolarity. Furthermore, the process of nation-building did not succeed in all countries and led to the emergence of states on the basis of an ethnic and not a political understanding of nation. It is argued in respect to especially Africa that the state is a product of colonial times and has only the semblance of a state after independence, which relies for the most part on repression. An analysis which comes closest to reality thus has to consider several factors: among others, ethnical as well as economical factors.[131]

Economical factors have played a catalytic role in some cases with respect to the provision of strategic rents. The trend of state failure has especially aggravated in Africa: in many cases, the inherited colonial state could not be transformed into a sustainable institution for development and nation-building. The differentiation of the society in a relatively autonomous state and an acquisitive society which acts according to free-market criteria

---

[129] Rittberger 2008a.
[130] Hirsch 2000: 333, cited in: Ruf 2003: 11.
[131] Ruf 2003: 24-27.

has been blocked, mostly by a bureaucratic elite with a marked rent mentality. Characteristic for this are the informalizing of politics (politicized ethnicity, clientelism, corruption) and economy (high importance of the informal sector). The ruinous consequences of the erosion of state functions are especially apparent in civil war states (Somalia, Liberia).[132] "A feature of such conflicts is", according to Boutros Boutros-Ghali, "the collapse of State institutions, especially the police and judiciary, with resulting paralysis of governance, a breakdown of law and order, and general banditry and chaos."[133] It also has an impact on how an international intervention for the resolution of an internal conflict has to be constituted: it "must extend beyond military and humanitarian tasks and must include the promotion of national reconciliation and the re-establishment of effective government."[134]

Summary

The structural conditions globalization and anarchy are set as constant factors: they describe the social reality of a new civil war and do not vary during the time span of a civil war. The systemic conditions globalization and anarchy determine, on the one hand, the ability of a state to hold the central authority over its territory: there is no central authority which has supremacy over the states in the international system and regulates the relations between states and within individual states; in particular, processing the negative effects of globalization (for example, connections between open war economies with international organised crime). For this reason, globalization and areas of limited or failed statehood are not subjected to any restrictions under the condition of anarchy. On the other hand, the structural conditions determine the manifestations of the features of new wars: for example, the extent to which the relations and activities of the conflict actors are transnationally or globally shaped and for which opportunities and restrictions those activities are liable to.

---

[132] Ruf 2003: 27f.
[133] Boutros-Ghali 1995: 9, cited in: Thürer 1995: 9.
[134] ibid: 9.

New wars often occur in states which pass through a process of state failure. State failure can be attributed to different causes: advanced by external encouragement of liberalization and privatization or the politics of patronage, proceeding from the government of the affected state.[135] State failure has an impact on the way a new civil war is conducted and financed and on the way it can be ended in the face of these possibilities and hindrances. In virtue of the loss of a central state authority, the war activities are marked by factional battles between rebel groups, which compete for political governance. The presence of natural resources like timber and easily extractable diamonds enables war actors to finance their war activities, independent from the assistance of other states, with the exploration and trading in these resources. The illegal trade in natural resources is, in turn, only possible because there is no central authority which can prohibit such trade, and transnational as well as international trade relations between war actors and trade partners abroad are often not monitored or prohibited (except, for example, the Kimberley Process).

Independent Variables

Nature of the Conflict

The variable nature of the conflict determines the degree of difficulty of the environment against which background a peace agreement is signed. The focus is on factors which constitute the conflict at the internal level and whose combined values determine the degree of difficulty of the conflict nature. The categories valuable natural resources and neighbouring states (with respect to financial support) cover the economic aspect of conflict: the conflict parties derive their financial means for their war activities from different sources. However, valuable natural resources and supporting neighbouring states are the two most significant economical sources for warring factions in new wars. "[N]o peace agreement has", according to Stedman, "been successfully implemented where there are valuable, easily

---

[135] Cf. Münkler 2002; Reno 1998.

41

marketable commodities such as gems or timber."[136] The presence of neighbouring states that support individual or several warring factions affects the peace process to the effect that they can oppose the peace agreement and continue their assistance to spoilers (warring factions that oppose a certain peace agreement and attempt to undermine it by the use of violence). The category neighbouring states can, on the one hand, constitute the potential or actual regionalization of an intra-state conflict. As the classification of the variable nature of the conflict centres on the internal and not the regional level, the external support is only conceived as one of the conflict parties' financial (and/or military) sources; thus, the focus is on the warring faction(s). The categories number of warring factions and distribution of power determine how the territory of a given state is divided: first, how many parties and, secondly, into how many parts (depending on the number of warring factions), also considering their respective sizes (determined by the extent of power held by the different warring factions). Furthermore, the proliferation of warring factions means that more actors have to be included in peace negotiations and the successive peace implementation, thus multiplying the number of interests and security fears that have to be considered by the mediating third parties. Some warring factions can exert more influence on the peace process than others because of their control of a large percentage of the contested territory, especially when the occupied territories contain easily exploitable valuable natural resources. The number of casualties – combatants as well as civilians – determines the intensity of the conflict: the more casualties a conflict entails, the higher is its intensity and the more difficult is its resolution due to the escalated stage of the conflict and hardened positions of the involved actors. Civilian casualties are included in this category as warring factions in new wars do not distinguish between combatants and civilians, and civilians increasingly become targets during intra-state conflicts.

---

[136] Stedman 2001b: 2.

Operationalization

The dimensions valuable natural resources, neighbouring states, number of conflict parties, casualties and distribution of power (Table 3.1) can take up different values, and thereby determine, whether a conflict nature is more easy or difficult for peace implementation. It applies: if three or more dimensions can be classified as difficult, then the conflict nature is to be defined as difficult. If less than three dimensions fall into the category difficult, then the nature of the conflict is to be rated as easy.

Table 3.1 Nature of the Conflict		
Nature of the Conflict	DIFFICULT	EASY
Valuable natural resources	Present Easily exploitable/lootable Moderately obstructable to unobstructable Geographically dispersed	Not present Difficult to exploit/unlootable Obstructable Geographically concentrated
Neighbouring states	Financial and/or military support of one or more conflict parties	No or termination of financial and/or military support of one or more conflict parties
Number of conflict parties	More than 2 conflict parties	2 conflict parties
Casualties (Combatants and civilians)	More than 1000 casualties	Less than 1000 casualties
Distribution of power	More than 50% of the territory under the control of a conflict party	Less than 50 % of the territory under the control of a conflict party

The more dimensions have the classification difficult, the more challenging is the nature of the conflict and the more difficult is the conflict settlement. If easily exploitable, geographically dispersed valuable natural resources are present in a given country and the warring factions are supported financially and/or militarily by neighbouring states, the higher are the benefits of the continuance of war due to financial gains and the less likely is a preference of peace to war by the warring factions. The more conflict parties are part of a conflict, the higher is the probability of the presence of a spoiler, which is not satisfied with the peace process and prefers hostilities to the state of peace (without regard to the potential costs of spoiling behaviour). The higher the number of combatant and civilian casualties is, the higher is the level of escalation of the conflict and the more difficult is the settlement of a conflict. This follows that the mediating and implementing third parties have to adopt strategies and measures which can measure up to the degree of difficulty of the conflict.[137]

Quality of the Peace Agreement Design

It is important for the explanation and assessment of the implementation of a peace agreement to investigate how the peace agreement itself is formulated and which provisions it includes. The quality of the design and the provisions of the peace agreement have consequences for peace implementation. This is because the lower the specification of sub-goals, guarantees and mechanisms for peace implementation, the lower is the quality of the peace agreement design and its provisions and the more unlikely is a successful implementation in a difficult conflict environment. A generally phrased agreement can have the advantage that the implementing third party has a certain freedom of interpretation with respect to the provisions during implementation difficulties and can, therefore, change tasks and time lines according to situations and resources without facing any major difficulties. Disadvantages, however, predominate: the conflict parties can interpret the peace agreement according to their interest and only implement the points which are conducive to them, if it was not clearly specified in the peace agreement and the conflict parties do not have to fear any measures in case of their violation of the agreement provisions. It can, furthermore, contribute to misunderstandings in regard to the chronological order of the various sub-goals, if the time schedule is inappropriately ascertained. In particular, the clear specification of the demobilization and disarmament phases is important because of the security interests of the combatants.

---

[137] Cf. Ramsbotham et al. 2005: 12: The hour glass model of Ramsbotham et al. depicts that conflict resolution strategies are more or less appropriate or possible for certain escalation or de-escalation stages.

Operationalization

In Table 3.2, the dimensions sub-goals, schedules, distribution of tasks, spoiler, future contentious issues, guarantees and included actors are presented as indicators of the variable quality of the peace agreement design. They can have different values and determine whether the quality of the peace agreement design and its provisions is high, medium or low. It applies: If four or more dimensions fall into the category high, then the quality of the peace agreement design is high. If less than four are classified as high but not more than one of the dimensions are judged as low, then the quality of the peace agreement design is considered as medium. If less than four are classified as high but more than one of the dimensions is judged as low, then the quality of the peace agreement design is low.

Table 3.2 Quality of the peace agreement design and its provisions			
Quality of the peace agreement design & its provisions	HIGH	MEDIUM	LOW
Sub-goals	Specification of the most important sub-goals	Specification of most of the important sub-goals	No specification of the important sub-goals
Schedules	Appropriate schedules	Problematic schedules	No schedules
Distribution of tasks	Tasks of the various parties are specified	Tasks of the various parties are partly specified	Tasks are not specified
Spoiler	Measures against spoiler	Threats against spoiler	No measures
Future contentious issues	Fora for the processing of future contentious issues are specified	Processing of future contentious issues are left abstract	No processing of future contentious issues
Guarantees	Specification of guarantees (security, power-sharing)	General provisions	No provisions
Included actors	Inclusion of all important conflict parties and civil society	Inclusion of all important conflict parties	Inclusion of not all important conflict parties

The more dimensions have the classification low, the lower is the quality of the peace agreement design. Thus, the less comprehensive and specific the peace agreement and its provisions is, the less likely is a successful peace implementation in a difficult conflict environment. If the most important sub-goals such as demobilization, disarmament and reintegration of combatants, the constitution of the transition government, the organisation of general elections, the institution of reforms and the regulation of the trade in natural resources are specified in the peace agreement, then the less contentious is the peace agreement during its implementation as the most important issues have been set down and agreed to by the warring factions before signing the peace agreement. In the case that new contentious issues arise during peace implementation, mechanisms are to be specified and instituted which immediately deal with arising disputes before they escalate and jeopardize the peace process. Furthermore, measures against spoilers have to be constituted in the peace agreement that apply in the case of a violation of the peace agreement and its provisions by a warring faction. One way of avoiding the presence or emergence of a spoiler is the inclusion of all relevant conflict parties in the peace negotiations; thus, preventing a potential disturbance of successive peace implementation. Representatives of civil society are also to be included in the peace process as the strengthening of civil society actors is important for the rebuilding of the country. They can counter-balance exaggerate demands of (ex-)combatants and provide a voice for the needs and fears of civilians. Therefore, if the combined values of the dimensions for the peace agreement design are high, the more likely is a successful implementation of the peace agreement. Nonetheless, a less comprehensive agreement with a low commitment of third parties can lead to a successful implementation in an easy conflict environment. It applies, however, for a difficult conflict environment: the more difficult the conflict nature is, the higher the quality of the peace agreement design and the stronger the engagement of the third parties has to be so that a peace agreement can be successfully implemented.

International Interest and Commitment

The variable international interest and commitment is defined as the support of peace implementation by the international community, which with regard to the value of its dimensions is more or less appropriate in dealing with a certain conflict in a more or less difficult conflict environment. A peace mission with a comprehensive mandate, appropriate provision of troops and resources can be more effective in a difficult conflict environment and can achieve more than an inappropriately equipped mission with observer status. The appropriate equipment and commitment of an internationally deployed mission depends, however, on whether the international interest is high enough towards a particular peace process, especially whether an influential state has a direct interest in the war-affected country and its peace implementation.[138] When there is no major international interest with regard to a particular civil war, then no appropriate reaction towards the termination of the war is likely. The timely provision of pledged assistance after the signing of the peace agreement is important to maintain the momentum of the peace negotiations and not to raise mistrust on the part of the conflict parties with regard to the implementability of the agreement. Furthermore, the taking up of measures against spoilers sends a signal to other actors that spoiler behaviour entails costs like, for example, the freezing of accounts.

Operationalization

The degree of international support (Table 3.3) is measured by means of the dimensions provided assistance, number of peacekeepers, resources, mandate, commitment and spoiler or by their respective scoring in a particular implementation phase. The dimensions can be evaluated as high, medium or low with respect to the international commitment. It applies: If four or more dimensions fall into the category high, then the international interest and commitment is high. If less than four are classified as high but not more than one of the dimensions is judged as low, then the international interest and commitment is to be

---

[138] Cf. Stedman 2001a/b.

categorized as medium. If less than four are assessed as high but more than one of the dimensions are judged as low, then the international interest and commitment is low.

Table 3.3	International interest and commitment		
International interest & commitment	HIGH	MEDIUM	LOW
Provided assistance	Timely provision of pledged assistance	Pledged assistance is provided later or reduced	Rhetorical support
Number of peacekeepers	Appropriate number of peacekeepers	Inappropriate number of peacekeepers	No peacekeepers
Resources	Appropriate resources	Inappropriate resources	No resources
Mandate	Comprehensive mandate, including peace enforcement	Non-comprehensive mandate, without peace enforcement	No mandate
Commitment	Long-term commitment	Withdrawal after elections	No commitment
Spoiler	Measures against spoilers	Threats against spoilers	No measures

The more dimensions have the classification low, the less engaging is the international interest and commitment in a given conflict and, consequently, the less difficult the conflict environment has to be in order for peace implementation to succeed under this condition of a low international commitment. If the pledged international assistance and an appropriate number of peacekeepers and resources is provided without delay shortly after the signing of a peace agreement, then there is a higher likelihood that the agreed ceasefire will not be violated by the warring factions, which could renege the peace process and lead to a relapse to large-scale violence. A timely deployment of a comprehensive, adequately resourced peace mission is thus important for the upkeep of the agreed-on ceasefire and the setting in of peace implementation. Additionally, the longer the time-span for the deployment of a peace mission is, the more likely is the full implementation of the sub-goals specified in the peace agreement and the more likely is a return to peaceful conditions. In the context of a new war, it is more likely that peace implementation and the succeeding peace consolidation is successful, if measures against spoilers are considered and instituted in the case of a violation of the peace agreement provisions as well as the continuous trade in natural resources for the financing of war activities is prohibited by the effecting of economic sanctions, which are to be in place until the completion of the reform of respective sectors.

Summary

The independent variables nature of the conflict, quality of the peace agreement design, and international interest and commitment are depicted as a triangle in Figure 1. Each of the variables is a necessary but not sufficient condition to explain the explanandum success vs. failure of peace implementation. The respective values of the independent variables have an effect on the success prospects of peace implementation. The three selected variables can, however, only explain the explanandum when they are considered together.

The respective indicators of the independent variables can assume different values (nature of the conflict: difficult vs. easy; quality of the peace agreement design, and international interest & commitment: high, medium, low) and, thereby, determine if the quality of the strategies or provisions are appropriate in regard to the degree of difficulty of the conflict. The features of the new wars are considered in the selection of the indicators of the respective independent variables as the concern of the study is to explain peace implementation in a new war. The indicators of conflict nature valuable natural resources and neighbouring states encompass the transnational or global character of new wars: conflict parties predominantly finance their war activities through the illegal trade in natural resources and are often financially and/or militarily supported by neighbouring states. Denationalization or privatization and asymmetry of warfare are reflected in the indicators number of conflict parties, number of casualties and distribution of power. The increased number of civilian casualties in comparison to that of combatants describes the loss of regulation and brutality of the new wars. There are often no battles between rebel groups but defenceless civilians are mutilated, raped, displaced, coerced into forced labour or recruitment, or killed in a most brutal way. The values of the indicators of quality of peace agreement design, and international interest and commitment consider whether and how far incentives and measures for the containment of spoiler behaviour are given or constituted in a peace process. A disincentive for spoiler behaviour can, for example, be the threat of sanctions[139] or the debarment from the transition government.

Each independent variable has to be seen in connection with the other variables. They are interdependent: depending on how one of the variables is coined, it has consequences for the values of the other variables. The relations between the independent variables can de described as follows: (1) the higher the quality of the peace agreement design, the more likely is a restrictive effect on the conflict nature; (2) the higher the international interest and commitment, the more likely is a high quality of the peace agreement design; and (3) the more difficult the conflict nature, the higher the degree of international commitment has to be so that a successful peace implementation can be achieved.

<u>Action Theory</u>

Cost-Benefit-Analysis of Actors

The values of the respective independent variables have consequences for the decision of the individual conflict parties whether they cooperate or not to peace implementation. The conflict parties are the central actors: They decide on whether the hostilities end or not, and the absence of hostilities is an important precondition for the succeeding of peace implementation. The most relevant, influential conflict parties have to be included in the peace negotiations, and their cooperation ensured through the provision of incentives (positive/negative). The conflict parties are considered as rational actors, which trade costs against benefits of the various courses of

---

[139] Concerning the application and effectiveness of sanctions, see Brzoska 2001; Wallensteen/Staibano 2005.

actions for the attainment of their goals. They are to choose the course of action which, from their perspective, presents the lowest costs but the highest benefits for their ends.

The conflict parties have the interest to secure their power position and influence that they have attained during the civil war: through the acquisition and control of territories, especially such, which are rich in valuable natural resources, the power position of a particular conflict party is strengthened in relation to other conflict parties. The conflict party attempts to secure this power position during peace negotiations and in the implementation phase through concessions of other conflict parties and guarantees by third parties.

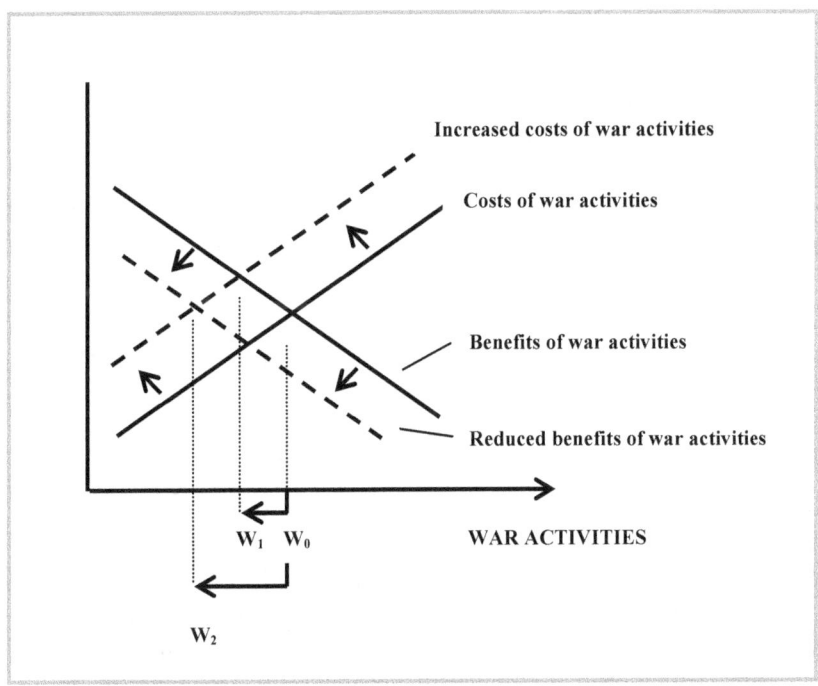

Figure 3.2   Cost-benefit-alteration of war activities[140]

The conflict parties have, furthermore, the goal to ensure their political and financial interests. Unless their interests and the physical survival of the respective conflict parties are guaranteed

---

[140] Cf. Frey 2008.

during the implementation phase, the conflict parties favour the continuation of hostilities over the costs of peace implementation. The conflict parties fear to be marginalised in peace implementation through the loss of military and financial securities (especially through demobilization and disarmament of their combatants, regulation of the extraction of and trade with natural resources) and, as a consequence, left defenceless to the spoiler behaviour of other conflict parties. Figure 3.2 depicts the alteration of costs and benefits with respect to war activities: W_0 represents the state of costs and benefits of war activities before any alteration to their scoring. It, thus, stands for how the conflict parties consider the costs and benefits of waging war, favouring the state of war to the state of peace. W_1 records increased costs of war activities, whilst W_2 depicts an additional alteration in the benefits – reduced benefits of war activities. Costs and benefits of war activities can be affected by measures and incentives (positive as well as negative) taken or provided by third parties, a change in the distribution of power between the conflict parties and/or by changes within a conflict party such as power struggles, change in leadership and intrafactional fragmentation.

The estimation of the costs and benefits of war activities are, furthermore, affected by a change in the evaluation of peace implementation. An alteration of the costs and benefits with regard to peace implementation can lead to a more or less likely preference of peace implementation to war activities by the conflict parties. In the Cost-benefit-alteration of peace implementation (Figure 3.3), P_0 represents the status of costs and benefits before their changed evaluation; P_1 depicts a state of increased benefits; and P_2 represents the point of junction of increased benefits and reduced costs of peace implementation. Peace implementation has, thus, become a more favourable option compared to the scoring of state P_0. The costs and benefits of peace implementation can be favourably altered by, for example, the introduction of positive incentives and provision of security and/or power-sharing guarantees by third parties. The costs and benefits of war activities vs. peace implementation are, however, to be considered as interdependent: the costs have to be lower and the benefits to be higher of peace implementation in comparison to the costs and benefits of war activities so that conflict parties choose the course of action cooperation in peace implementation.

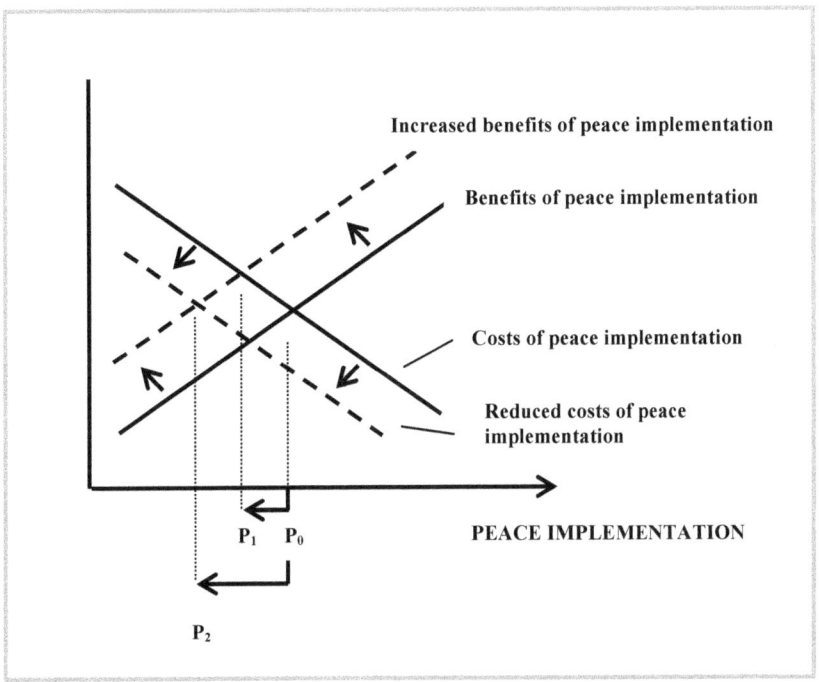

Figure 3.3   Cost-benefit-alteration of peace implementation[141]

Course of Action

The preferences and expectations of actors are dependent on the opportunities and constraints of social reality and the actions of other actors (other conflict parties, mediating third parties and neighbouring states). According to the scoring of the three independent variables, the conflict parties either choose the course of action H1 Cooperation or H2 Non-cooperation in the implementation phase. In the face of insecurity and incomplete information in regard to the selection of a course of action by the opposing conflict party/parties, the conflict parties are more likely to cooperate in a difficult conflict environment, if a high international assistance is provided for peace implementation.

---

[141] Cf. Frey 2008.

The appropriateness of strategies and incentives by third parties determine to a large extent which course of action is more attractive for the conflict parties. The raising of the costs for the continuation of hostilities by, for example, the threat or implementation of sanctions against spoilers and the simultaneous raising of the benefits of cooperation by the provision of guarantees can influence the costs-benefits-estimation of the conflict parties in such an extent that they prefer H1 to H2 and thus cooperate.

It applies: as the more difficult the conflict nature, the higher the quality of the peace agreement design and the international commitment have to be such that (1) the fears of the conflict parties of betrayal and marginalization can be minimized or removed through guarantees and commitment by third parties; and (2) the preferences and expectations of the conflict parties are influenced through incentives in such a way that it results in an adjustment of preferences from H2 to H1. From this it follows that, the lower the costs and the higher the benefits for the course of action H1 Cooperation in the implementation phase are from the perspective of the conflict parties for the securing of their political and financial interests, the more likely they will cooperate in regard to the implementation of a peace agreement.

Dependent Variable

Success vs. Failure of Peace Implementation

The conflict parties select the course of action which yields them, as rational profit-maximizing actors, the highest profit. It is assumed that the respective conflict parties are under the same conditions so that, for example, in the case of a spoiler behaviour conflict party A would be subjected to the same measures as conflict party B. This means for the aggregation of the chosen courses of action of the diverse conflict parties that, in the case of a high quality of the peace agreement design and a high international commitment in the context of a difficult conflict environment, the conflict parties prefer the course of action H1 to course of action H2. The conflict parties thus cooperate under these conditions in regard to peace implementation, and the result is the successful implementation of the peace agreement. In the reverse case, it implies that under the conditions difficult conflict nature, low quality of the peace agreement design and low international commitment, the conflict parties decide for the course of action H2 Non-cooperation, and the result is a relapse to extended violence, which can develop into a full-fledged war within a very short time.

The ideal case successful implementation of a peace agreement has again consequences on social reality: a cornerstone for the (re)establishment of state structures is laid through the implementation of peaceimplementing measures, which, in contrast to the process of state failure during the civil war, initiate a process of state-building.

Operationalization

Different operationalizations of success can be found in writings on war termination: termination of hostilities[142]; stability for five years[143]; ending of war on a self-sustaining basis so that the implementing third parties can withdraw without the danger of a relapse into war[144]; probability of the renewed outbreak of war; mandate accomplishment.[145] The success of peace implementation is here hinged on if and how far the peace agreement was implemented. It can be noted in regard to this operationalization that it is too fixed on the peace agreement and does not consider whether agreements can, on the one hand, be comprehensive and, on the other hand, too general or inadequately formulated. However, the phase shortly after the signing of the peace agreement is assessed and not long-term peace consolidation and, therefore, the immediate implementation of the peace agreement provisions are used as the point of measuring success. The quality of a peace agreement – comprehensive, appropriate vs. too general, inappropriate – is, secondly, incorporated in the indicators of the independent variable quality of peace agreement design: different kinds of

---

[142] Hampson 1996.
[143] Hartzell et al. 2001.
[144] Stedman et al. 2002.
[145] See also Stedman et al. 2002: Chapter 1.

peace agreements can, thus, be adequately assessed and differentiated from others. The used operationalization of success vs. failure of peace implementation covers the various stages of war up to the implementation of the peace agreement: the variance of the dependent variable can, thereby, depict the diverse outcomes of different implementation processes. Thus, two or more peace implementations can be compared with each other which, for example, take place at different points in time within the same country. The operationalization of the dependent variable is as follows: (1) success: implementation of the peace agreement; (2) partial success: (a) partial implementation of the peace agreement; (b) stabilization of a negative peace; (3) failure: (a) relapse to large-scale violence; (b) war.

Several steps are necessary for the evaluation of peace implementation: The first step is to analyze which sub-goals were specified in a particular peace agreement. It is then to be ascertained if and how far the respective sub-goals were implemented during the implementation phase. Table 3.4 lists the most important sub-goals[146], which are to be ideally included in an agreement in the context of a new war, and the degree of their implementation. The degree of processing of the sub-goals is tabulated on the basis of the categories high, medium and low: the sub-goal reintegration is, for example, set as high when it was completed during the implementation phase.

The most important sub-goals are, in turn, differentiated with respect to their priority for peace implementation: demobilization, disarmament, power sharing or political participation, and the organization of elections are of the highest priority after the signing of a peace agreement. They are those factors which are important for the trust of the conflict parties in the peace process: the ensuring of their security (for example, the disarming of all conflict parties at the same point in time) and political future in times of peace (for example, the possibility of political participation and potential winning of general elections as incentives) has priority for them. The other factors reintegration, trade in natural resources and reforms take up a less prominent position: they are of importance for the mid-term and

---

[146] See also Table 3.2 Quality of the peace agreement design and its provisions.

long-term success of the peace process and are to be instituted during peace implementation. The differentiation into two categories of priority is necessary for the measuring of success: (1) success: the implementation of the four sub-goals of top priority fall into the category high. The other sub-goals are instituted and partly implemented during peace implementation; (2) partial success: (a) less than four of the sub-goals of top priority are implemented, and the other sub-goals are only partially or not implemented; (b) stabilization of a negative peace: a cease fire and less than 25 casualties per year are considered as negative peace; and (3) failure: (a) a relapse to large-scale violence is recorded with more than 25 but less than 1000 casualties per year; (b) more than 1000 casualties per year are a sign of the renewed outbreak of war.

Table 3.4 Implementation of the most important sub-goals during peace implementation			
Peace implementation	HIGH	MEDIUM	LOW
Demobilization	Completed	Partly implemented	No demobilization
Disarmament	Completed	Partly implemented	No disarmament
Reintegration	Completed	Partly implemented	No reintegration
Trade in natural resources	Regulation implemented	Partial regulation	No regulation
Power sharing or political participation	Power sharing or political participation implemented	Power sharing or political participation partly implemented	No power sharing or political participation
Reforms	Institution and implementation of reforms	Partial institution and implementation of reforms	No institution of reforms
Elections	Organization and conduct of free and fair elections	Deficient organization and conduct of elections	No elections

Summary

The generated theory model, on the one hand, explicates the interrelations between a given structure and the behaviour of actors, and, on the other hand, amplifies the challenges for implementing peace in the setting of a new war. The actors are subject to constraints and opportunities, which, consequently, influence their preference for a certain course of action. If the actors choose cooperation over non-cooperation in peace implementation as the most beneficial course of action for the attainment of their goals, then the aggregated selection of cooperation by the actors has a favourable impact on the macro level - success of peace implementation. The new war peculiarities are considered in the context factors as well as in the dimensions of the independent variables: anarchy, globalization and failing or failed state constitute the structural conditions in which a new war is set. They especially emphasize the limited ability of a central authority (either a supra-national or national authority) to manage a conflict which is denationalized due to its transnational and international connections; thus, embodying the characteristics of a new war. The independent variables nature of the conflict, quality of the peace agreement design, and international interest and commitment are designed to encompass the internal, transnational and international dimensions of a new war: they incorporate the proliferation of private actors on all levels, the financing of new war activities through the illegal trade in valuable natural resources and provided assistance by neighbouring states, the consequential institution of measures restricting the illegal trade in natural resources, and the increasing tactic of war actors to use civilians as prime targets, which in turn have to be involved in the peace process to encourage the normalization of relations between (ex-)combatants and civilians. Thus, the theory model amplifies the concept of new wars as it makes the ascribed features of a new war more specific and brings structural conditions and motives of actors into context with each other. Success or failure of peace implementation can, hence, be explained in a new type of war in applying the theory model on processes of peace implementation in contemporary intra-state conflicts.

A good theory, among other criteria, is one that is clearly framed: first, it fashions its variables from concepts that the theorist has clearly defined and, secondly, it includes a full outline of the theory's explanation as "[i]t does not leave us wondering how A causes B."[147] Theories that are based on causal mechanisms are thus more well-grounded or adequate in providing a better understanding and more complete picture of reality by showing the process from X to Y than theories that state that Y follows X regularly. The adduced process of causing can, on the one hand, contribute to a better and more precise testing of the theories and, on the other hand, be validated on the basis of reality.[148] In the study, the underlying concepts of the theory model – peace implementation and new wars – are clearly defined, and the theory model and formulated hypotheses provide a full outline of how a successful or failed peace implementation is effected. The causal mechanisms linking the independent variables with respective high, 'favourable' values to the dependent variable with value successful peace implementation can be portrayed in an arrow diagram (Figure 3.4).

The theoretical model depicts that the structural conditions lead to a certain action of the agents, here either cooperation or non-cooperation in peace implementation. Margaret Archer's morphogenetic cycle amplifies that structure and agency "are like two distinct strands which intertwine with one another", which can be temporally differentiated: structure predate agency whereby agency then causes a change of the structure.[149] According to Little[150], every social scientific theory with the emphasis on explanation has to be able to consider structure as well as agency. The subject-matter of the actor-structure-debate is the relation of agency and structure in the generation and explanation of social practice. Individualism alleges that social practice and social structures are fundamentally a result of the interaction of individual actions and

---

[147] Van Evera 1997: 19.
[148] Schimmelpfennig 1995: 251ff.
[149] Archer 1996; cited in: McAnulla 2002: 285f.
[150] Little et al. 1993: 104; cited in: Schimmelpfennig 1995: 253.

can thus be reduced to the agency of actors. Structuralism, on the other hand, assumes that the goals and actions of actors are imminently determined by their surrounding social structures. Structurationism, in turn, claims that agency and structure constitute, mark and transform each other: there would be no actors without structures as those provide them with a social identity and social roles; there would be no structures without actors as they are only created and reproduced by agency.[151]

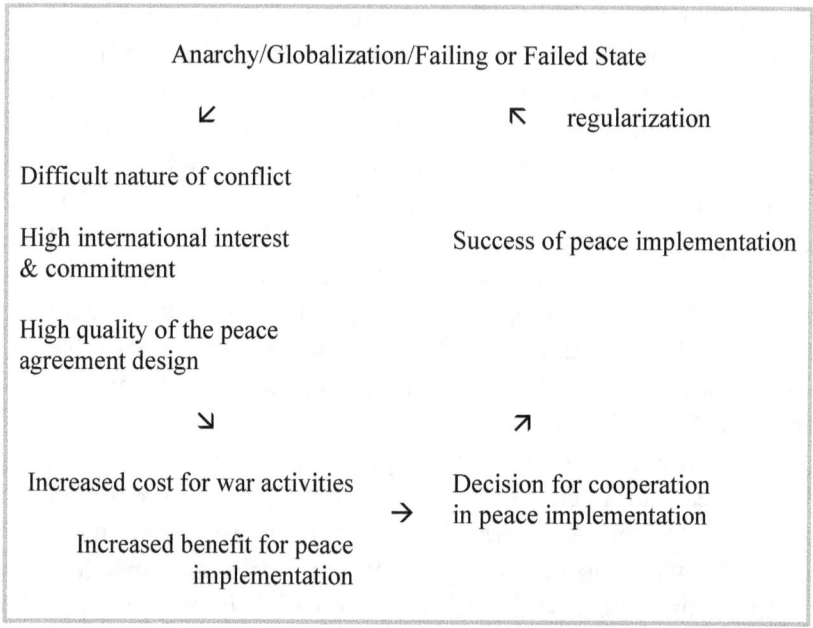

Figure 3.4   Causal mechanisms of successful peace implementation

Despite including the structural level in structural individualism, rational choice theory emphasizes the decisional level as the actors fundamentally decide whether they choose course of action A or B and thereby influence the outcome at the macro level. The problem of individualism, thus, can be assigned to the chosen theory model. However, the structural constraints and opportunities affecting the actors are amplified in the generated theory model as their respective values at given time t_1 have a different effect on the actors' preferences, interests and decisions

---

[151] Schimmelpfennig 1995: 254ff.

than at given time t_2. The interactions and mutual conditioning of structure and agency are elaborated so that the causal mechanisms leading from the independent variables to the dependent variable are made visible and contribute to a thorough analysis of the selected case study.

Different levels of analysis are, furthermore, built into the theory model: systemic, sub-systemic and individual levels of analysis. However, the level-of-analysis problem – the inducing of theory building defects due to the alternating between different levels of analysis during a theoretical statement[152] – is attended to through the following measures: first, the dependent and independent variables are both set at the sub-systemic or macro level (whilst the action theory is on the individual or micro level); secondly, the context factors at the systemic and sub-systemic levels respectively are considered as constant as they present structural conditions which set in before the considered points of analysis at a particular time t and, thus, do not have a direct influence on the causal process from the independent variables to the dependent variable. Due to the complexity of the theory model and the explanandum (value of peace implementation), it can, nonetheless, not be avoided to include dimensions and respective indicators of different levels in the variables, such as, for example, international factors like sanctions and neighbouring states: they are included to depict their effect on the actors and their decision to cooperate or not towards peace implementation; thus, they point back to the macro level of the dependent variable through the interaction of aggregated courses of action and structure. According to Schimmelpfennig, in complex events such as war or revolution, causal mechanisms of different types – structural, dispositional, interactional – as well as several mechanisms of the same type (for example, structures of the environment and of the units) operate sequentially. This implies that every theory, capturing societal events, has to be an aggregated theory.[153]

---

[152] Schimmelpfennig 1995: 258.
[153] ibid: 260.

Case Study

In the preceding section a theory model was generated which can explain success or failure of peace implementation in the context of a new war. The factors which were identified in war termination literature as significant in explaining success or failure in peace implementation were considered in the generation of the theory model whilst the assumptions of the concept of new wars are incorporated in the selection of the variables and their operationalization. According to van Evera, a theory-generating thesis presents new hypotheses which can use examples for the purpose of their validation and exemplification:

> "A theory-proposing dissertation advances new hypotheses. A deductive argument for these hypotheses is advanced. Examples may be offered to illustrate these hypotheses and to demonstrate their plausibility, but strong empirical tests are not performed."[154]

The generated theory concept is not subjected to a theory test in the context of this study but is illustrated by means of a real problem which has not found much attention in literature on war termination. It is the goal to be able to explain a peace process in its various outcomes (from failed to successful) in a new war. The research work cannot assert to be theoretically generalizable as only the strengths and weaknesses in the application of the generated theory on a single-case study can be presented, and no comprehensive theory test is conducted. This research design, however, enables a more profound, comprehensive investigation of a single-case study and the highlighting of the particularities of a specific peace process which would not be possible in a quantitative study. The generated theory model is to specify how "certain conditions change over time" in the selected peace process(es), and the selected time intervals are to "reflect the presumed stages at which the changes should reflect themselves"[155]. In order to reflect the different stages in a

---

[154] Van Evera 1997: 89.
[155] Yin 2003: 42.

particular case study, a longitudinal[156] study is conducted with three interfaces, which means that three points of analysis are selected which represent the three most important peace agreements along the time frame of an overall peace process in a particular war-affected country. Thus, it is not a holistic single-case study as it has several embedded units of analysis[157] – a study of several cases at the subunit level. According to Yin[158], "[t]he subunits can often add significant opportunities for extensive analysis, enhancing the insights into the single case". The larger, holistic aspects of the case, however, have to be kept in view and the relationship of the subunits to the overall case – in this case the specific peace implementation phases to the overall peace process – has to be indicated.

Case Selection

The single-case study Liberia is selected as an "outlier"[159] case which is poorly explained by existing explanatory approaches and a contemporary problem of the real world which is rarely and insufficiently attended to in war termination literature.[160] The selection of a peace process in one country instead of a comparison of peace processes in different countries is advantageous for the assessment of the peace implementation phases because the different phases can be compared more easily as they are subjected to the same or similar conditions – for example in respect to the conflict parties (command structure and operation) and nature of conflict (presence of natural resources and collapsed state institutions). The three points of interception of the longitudinal study are chosen as such that they encompass the three most significant peace agreements Cotonou, Abuja I and II, and Accra and their respective implementation, which, in turn, differ in their values of the dependent and independent variables: the value of the dependent variable – success or failure of peace implementation – varies widely with the values of the

---

[156] According to Yin (2003: 42), the study of a "longitudinal case" is defined as "studying the same single case at two or more different points in time".
[157] See also Yin 2003: 42ff.
[158] ibid: 46.
[159] Van Evera 1997: 86.
[160] See also Chapter Two for the relevance of selected case study.

independent variables from peace implementation phase I to peace implementation phase II up to peace implementation phase III.[161]

---

[161] See also van Evera 1997: 61f. According to van Evera (1997: 82), one is to select "cases with large within-case variance in the value on the independent variable, dependent variable, or condition variable across time and space".

FOUR

Implementation of Peace Agreements in Liberia

Liberia: Background

Liberia is "an aberration and an archetype: in the African context, its political history is unique, yet its contemporary record is typical of other African states".[162] Its uniqueness stems from its lack of a colonial legacy, despite its "quasi-colonial period in which the American Colonization Society (ACS), an American pseudohumanitarian association governed by white American slave owners, ruled dominion (1822-1847)"[163]. In 1847, the freed North American slaves, who were resettled by the ACS along the present-day Monrovia coast, declared Liberia as an independent republic. However, the majority of indigenous village-states remained independent as the indigenous groups had no interest in becoming subjects of the settlers' republic; thus, the founding of the republic provoked several wars with indigenous groups over political legitimacy, economic resources and land.[164]

The republic was modelled on the presidential system of the United States but came to be ruled as a one-party state under the control of the True Whig Party. The Americo-Liberian elite (descendants of the freed slaves), which controlled the True Whig Party, established an oligarchy, which was centred on the exclusion and oppression of the 16 ethnical groups forming the indigenous local population. Although comprising over 95% of

---

[162] Levitt 2005: 182.
[163] ibid: 182.
[164] ibid: 3-8.

65

the population, the indigenous peoples were treated as second-class citizens and were excluded from decision-making processes affecting their lives. The autocratic system was based on a system of patronage, with leaders dispensing favours and positions to associates. Its survival relied on a world market-oriented economy with the export of Liberia's resources, made up primarily by rubber, timber, iron ore and diamonds. Leaders amassed great fortunes by extracting national resources, whilst the general population lived in dire poverty.[165]

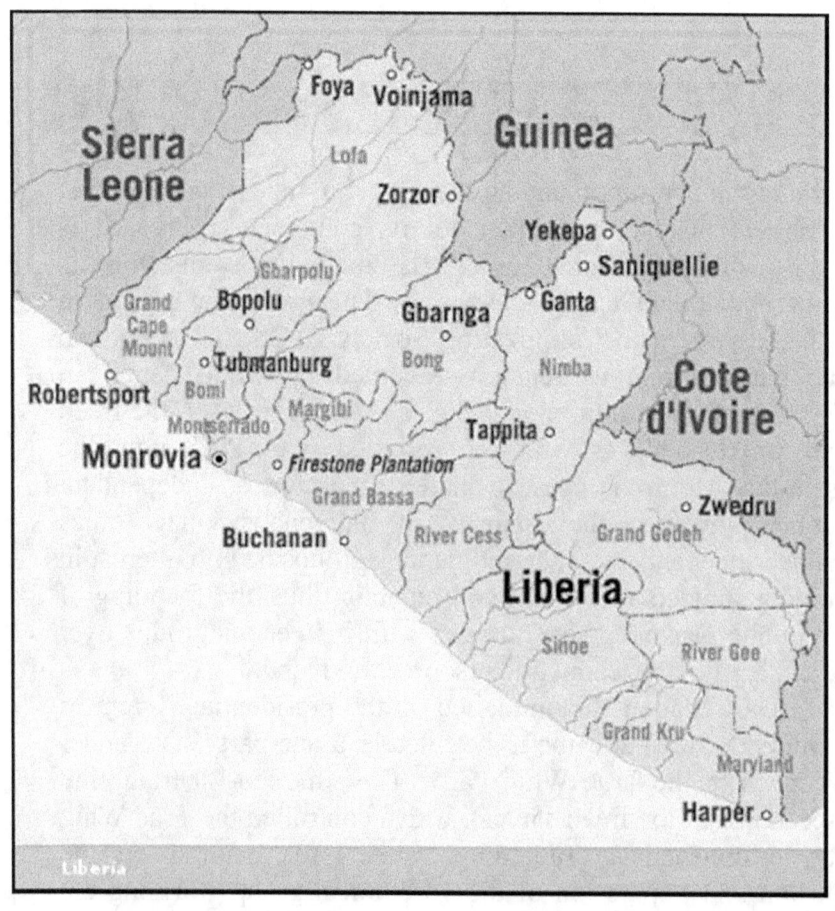

Map 4.1   Liberia[166]

---

[165] Woyke 2004: 172; Levitt 2005: 3-8; Adebajo 2002a: 45; Sesay: 11f., in: Accord 1996.
[166] International Crisis Group: Liberia.

This situation improved to some extent during the rule of William Tubman (1944-71), in which his Open Door Policy appeased indigenous Liberians by giving them a larger political stake in the country and by removing restrictive property rights qualifications. These policies were, however, only instituted to stabilize the settler's oligarchy, not abolishing its political and economical domination. The Liberian Legislature under Tubman adopted laws that "gave foreign investors full freedom of entry and repatriation of the capital and profits".[167] It created employment opportunities and development in the interior to many indigenous Liberians. It, however, also led to an increased foreign economic domination of Liberia's economy, which reached its culmination during Taylor's regime. Tubman's authoritarian style of suppressing full political and economical participation to both settlers and indigenous peoples, which were not part of his patronage network, created many enemies for him. During his later reign, Tubman took increasingly extreme measures to secure his position in power.[168]

William Tolbert (1971-80) continued to pursue integrationist policies, sought to appease the segments of society disillusioned during Tubman's reign, dismantled Tubman's extensive patronage network and replaced it with his loyalists. By 1971, Liberia's economic development had slowed down due to a decreased international demand for iron ore and rice during global recession. Amid growing economic problems, Tolbert had to resort to coercion and surveillance tactics to deal with unprecedented political challenges that developed inside and outside the oligarchy. The price increase on rice and imprisonment of protesters were mere triggers for the latent political crisis to culminate in the coup d'état of 1980.[169]

---

[167] Liebenow: 72; cited in: Levitt 2005: 186.
[168] Woyke 2004: 172; Levitt 2005: 184-190; Adebajo 2002a: 45; Sesay: 11f., in: Accord 1996.
[169] Woyke 2004: 172; Levitt 2005: 191-197; Adebajo 2002a: 45; Sesay: 11f., in: Accord 1996.

Figure 4.1   Samuel Doe[170]

In April 1980, seventeen officers led by Samuel Kanyon Doe attacked the Executive Mansion, assassinated President Tolbert and seized power. Samuel Doe claimed to have carried out the coup to liberate the masses from poverty and corruption, depicted in the name of his junta – the 'People's Redemption Council' (PRC). His coercive rule, however, made him unpopular with the masses, initially supportive of the overthrow of the Tolbert regime. Being wary of himself being ousted in a military coup, Doe invested heavily in creating a loyal military establishment, and arrested, forced into exile or assassinated potential rivals to his rule. Despite having inherited a collapsing economy, Doe continued the tradition of extracting economic resources for the elite's benefit.[171] In the mid-1980s, under pressure from the United States, Doe made attempts to re-establish civilian rule: the established constitutional and election oversight structures were, however, severely compromised by Doe's control.[172] The rigged presidential elections of 1985 led to several military challenges to Doe's regime; most significantly, the failed military coup of General Thomas Quiwonkpa, a Gio from Nimba county and former commander of Doe's army, in November 1985. In retaliation, Doe's mostly Krahn soldiers massacred a reported 3,000 Gios and Manos in Nimba County and Monrovia in late 1985. This episode set the stage for the exploitation of ethnic rivalries which found its culmination in the resulting civil wars.[173] The "combination of widespread corruption under the Doe regime, the precipitous decline in revenues from Liberia's main exports (rubber, timber, and iron ore), and the cessation of U.S. economic assistance", argues

---

[170] BBC 2009a.
[171] Woyke 2004: 172; Levitt 2005: 197-202; Adebajo 2002a: 45.
[172] Levitt 2005: 200.
[173] Adebajo 2002a: 45f.

Adekey Adebajo, "proved disastrous to Doe"[174], which culminated in Charles Taylor's 1989 invasion.

A background on Liberia's history is significant for the analysis of its civil wars of the 20th and 21st centuries and resulting peace processes as "Liberia's legacy of violent conflict is inextricably linked to its traditions of nationalism and authoritarianism"[175]. The authoritarian political apparatus instituted by the ACS in 1822 permanently shaped the socio-political order responsible for the institutionalization of ethno-political conflict with varying levels of violence: first of all, between the settlers and indigenous groups 1822-1980, and then, after Doe's coup d'état, among all Liberians 1980-2003.[176]

Liberia: A 'New' Type of War

Ayoob "observes a cyclical relationship between state failure, precipitated by a lack of legitimate authority, and internal conflict."[177] This cyclical relationship is applicable to Liberia – the authoritative repressive regimes under Americo-Liberian rule, the further decline of formal institutions under Doe, the building opposition against the Doe regime, the rise of Charles Taylor, the complete collapse of the state with the assassination of Doe, the legitimized operation of warlord politics following Taylor's election, fulminating in the second civil war. The growth of the shadow state ultimately weakened important formal institutions, including the military, created widespread opposition to the incumbent regimes and served as the source of its own collapse. Liberia's high dependence on primary commodity exports also made it more vulnerable to internal conflict as they could be used to finance armed conflict. The internal conflict, however, only became possible because of the low capacity of the state to counter challenges to its authority.[178]

---

[174] Adebajo 2002a: 46.
[175] Levitt 2005: 8.
[176] ibid: 8.
[177] Cater: 27, in: Ballentine/Sherman 2003.
[178] Cf. ibid: 28.

Liberia's state failure was not a short-term phenomenon but a long-term process. The policies of preceding governments and their exclusionary, authoritarian style of governance as well as simultaneous global political and financial conditions affecting state performance were the foundation for Samuel Doe's own policies, exacerbating the failing of state functions.[179] Liberia's state failure can thus not be equated with the incursion of National Patriotic Front of Liberia (NPFL) rebels in December 1989 and the destructive impact of the ensuing civil war. Moreover, it is questionable whether Liberia ever fulfilled all three state functions as for decades only a small fraction of Liberians – Americo-Liberians – had the right to vote and the concerns of the majority of Liberians – indigenous Liberians – were not adhered to by the elite. Thus the legitimacy of the respective governments was limited to a small percentage of the population despite being internationally recognized as Liberia's sovereign authority. With respect to sovereign authority, the elite only concentrated on the governing of the capital Monrovia, neglected the development of the hinterland and its inhabitants and condoned the displacement of local inhabitants by foreign companies in concessionary areas.

The coup of 1980 ended the privileges of the ruling oligarchy, led to the emergence of new political and economical constellations, and the development of politicized ethnicity. Samuel Doe's military rule can, however, largely be perceived as the continuance of the Americo-Liberian self-destructive project of authoritarian rule.[180] Despite being the first indigenous Liberian president, Samuel Doe failed to promote societal cohesion, instead relying on support from his Krahn ethnic tribe. The rigged elections of 1985, the policy of repression and poor provision of services contributed to the lack of legitimacy of Doe's regime, nullifying its acceptance as a source of identity. As the organization of decision-making, the state was inoperative as all power was concentrated in the hands of President Doe. Due to economic shortfalls[181] (external factors like the withdrawal of U.S. aid, the decline in world market prices for Liberia's export

---

[179] Cf. Zartman 1995: 5.
[180] Korte 1997: 58.
[181] Korte 1997: 64f.; Reno 2004: 118.

commodities and increase of import prices; internal factors like corruption, financial misfeasance, lack of economic management by the state, ruinous privatisation of the state and parastatal infrastructural institutions), the state was less able in providing basic services to the populace, thus affecting its support from as well its imposition of control over its citizens. Exemplary for the contraction of the Liberian economy are figures from the late 1980s: alone from 1988 to 1989, the official GDP fell from $1,038,300,000.00 billion to $786,300,000.00.[182] The developments of 1989 – deficit financing, administrative increase of the rice price, and stoppage of development projects – are indicators for the prevalent social potential of pauperization. It resulted in the expansion of the informal sector, the impoverishment of the population, the increased formation of slums and increase in crime.[183]

As a territory, the state did not act as a security guarantor: the regime under Doe focused on its own survival by the creation of multiple security institutions and intimidation of potential challengers to its reign rather than on the protection of its citizens. Doe "actively asserted personal control and attempted to impose his directives on others by force"[184], which alienated even close associates. According to Reno, "the collapse of government institutions and the emergence of hostilities constituting Liberia's internal war were integrally connected"[185]. As the progressively violent rule of Doe contributed to the emergence of dissidents, it in turn hastened the collapse of state institutions. Whilst Doe's reign and the following civil war destroyed the previous Americo-Liberian-imposed order, "it left in its place only more corruption, interethnic hatreds, rule of the gun, and fear and physical destruction"[186]. The likes of Charles Taylor saw the use of violent means as the only option of ending Doe's military rule. With Charles Taylor's forces controlling most of the country's territory, the assassination of Samuel Doe and the emergence of

---

[182] Nation Master.
[183] Korte 1997: 65.
[184] Reno 2004: 118.
[185] ibid.
[186] Lowenkopf 1995: 101.

anti-NPFL factions, the structures of the state eventually collapsed in autumn 1990.[187]

Figure 4.2   Charles Taylor – rebel, president, defendant[188]

The 1997 election of Charles Taylor as president did not lead to a change of policies but left the pre-war conditions intact, which confirms Reno's statement that "insurgents-turned-rulers continue practices and perpetuate grievances that led to war in the first place"[189]. Just as the preceding regimes, Taylor's regime made use of violence for personal aggrandizement and the control of the populace. With respect to Zartman's state functions, Taylor's regime could not even claim a monopoly over coercion as the minimal function of the state (in the tradition of Max Weber) because it only provided security to people whose activities contributed to the personal enrichment of the regime. Taylor thus "behaved more like a private entrepreneur than a ruler of a state, though his claim of sovereignty and his international recognition as a legitimate interlocutor in the process of conflict resolution provided him with the façade of a state behind which to conduct his operations"[190]. Taylor's regime, for example, qualified for debt relief under the Highly Indebted

---

[187] Korte 1997: 65f.
[188] BBC 2009b.
[189] Reno 2004: 116.
[190] ibid.

Poor Country (HIPC) initiative without having, on one hand, demonstrated any internal capacity to service the country's debts and, on the other hand, shown any commitment to providing basic services such as security or electricity to its populace. The official budget of Liberia under Taylor reflected high expenditures for security operations for the stabilization of the incumbent regime, whilst minimal social services were provided by the non-governmental sector than the state. Revenues for the national budget were primarily derived from taxes on foreign logging operations, fees from the Liberian maritime registry programme and excise taxes, although not all national resources reached national coffers.[191]

The advantage of sovereignty for the former warlord, was that, the position as "internationally accepted" head of state enabled him to eliminate rivals who competed for power and resources during the war. Furthermore, the internal lack of capacity reduced the danger of subordinates using state agencies to build alternative power bases and appropriating state assets without Taylor's authorization. Taylor created various security agencies for his own protection[192] and passed executive orders for all state revenues to be under his personal control. Reno argues that the negotiation with faction leaders and simultaneous exclusion of societal groups protects those leaders from having to provide services and engage in normal political activity for the attraction of popular support during peace times. Elections were thus not efficient in creating this new relationship: available resources enabled Taylor's regime to continue replicating and spreading to neighbouring countries the conditions of state collapse prevalent under Doe's regime and cause for Liberia's first civil war. The resolution of a war, resulting from state collapse, thus lies in rebuilding civil government than focusing on elections and the cessation of war activities.[193]

---

[191] Reno 2004: 127-135.
[192] ibid: 127f., 135.
[193] ibid: 136f.

Figure 4.3   Destroyed infrastructure in Buchanan, 2001[194]

Liberia's civil war took place in an environment which is marked by the subversion of the state's monopoly on the use of force: the state is replaced as the main actor of war by the emergence of private actors, challenging the state's authority. As the state broke apart in 1990, "its centre of gravity sub-divided and passed into the hands of sub-state actors"[195], which were not "politicians and statesmen accustomed to the use of power, but traders, petty criminals, and religious bigots"[196]. It resulted in "a state of anarchy and the total breakdown of law and order in Liberia"[197]. The successive interim governments could not maintain security without the assistance of the regional intervention force ECOMOG: the power devolved from the capital into the hinterland – into the hands of contending warring factions. The faction leaders controlled the areas held by them, exploiting the locally existing resources and holding the local population captive. Charles Taylor, for example, established "a rival capital, Gbarnga, with its own currency, radio station, police, hospital, and an embryonic crude government emanating from Taylor's villa, which communicated both internally to his subordinate commanders and to the world beyond" [198]. A successful peace process would have "stripped the warlords of their military

---

[194] Global Witness 2001d: 4.

[195] Alao et al. 1999: 116.

[196] ibid: 115.

[197] Communiqué of the ECOWAS Standing Mediation Committee, 7 August 1990, in: Weller 1994: 73.

[198] Alao et al. 1999: 116f.

power, their opportunities for trade and extortion, and their control over a relatively down-trodden civil population"[199].

Figure 4.4 Liberian child soldiers[200]

---

[199] Alao et al. 1999: 118.
[200] Global Witness 2005d: 12.

The privatisation of violence became particularly possible because warfare in a new war is relatively cheap due to the predominant use of light weapons and the deployment of child soldiers. The warring factions received a rapid expansion of their membership during the civil war and, in varying degrees, changed in character and organization over the conflict, for example, the NPFL "began the war as a loose coalition of former soldiers, "radical" intellectuals, politicians, exiles, and refugees hostile to Doe's dictatorship"[201], including Burkinabè, Sierra Leonean and Gambian mercenaries. By 1996 NPFL's original fighting core of 168 had increased to "over 15,000 fighters of widely different ages and levels of training, skills, and discipline"[202]. According to Funmi Olonisakin, "[B]etween 15,000 and 20,000 children, including young women and girls, were eventually used in various capacities by the different armed factions"[203]. The reprisals by Doe's Armed Forces of Liberia (AFL) against perceived rebel sympathizers in Nimba and Lofa Counties left many children orphaned, which made them susceptible to rebel recruitment to either avenge the deaths of their families or attain security and gain access to food. With the progression of war and the proliferation of armed forces, the competition for new recruits intensified, which led to the forceful recruitment of youth. "Press-ganged, psychologically primed, and dosed with cane-juice, marijuana, and other narcotic substances, many of these children committed cruel atrocities against innocent civilians"[204] – including members of their own families and communities. This in turn bound the youths further to the armed groups, hampering the return to their communities after the end of hostilities.

---

[201] Abdullah/Rashid: 181f., in: Adebajo/Rashid 2004.
[202] ibid.
[203] Olonisakin: 248, in: Adebajo/Rashid 2004.
[204] ibid: 249.

Figure 4.5 Militia members[205]

"The combatants wore frightening costumes, awarded themselves high-sounding military titles, and adopted terrifying noms de guerre depending on their deeds, self-perception, and images derived from the popular media and movies"[206], which Abdullah and Rashid attribute to the desire of combatants to terrorize others as well as indiscriminate looting. The way one thinks of Liberia's war is "strongly influenced by images of chaos and random violence"[207] due to the abandonment of all rules and conventions of war from the onset of the incursion, with civilians forming the main target of warfare. Approximately 200,000 people, forming about 8 percent of the Liberian population, died in fighting or massacre, and more than half of the country's population became refugees.[208] Jeffrey Goldberg described it as "a war without purpose in a country without identity" that was terrorized by "teenagers in NBA T-shirts".[209] Already in August 1990, the fighting had caused a high level of destruction of property coupled with the various warring factions' participation in the massacre of thousands of innocent civilians, including foreign nationals, women and children, "some of whom had sought sanctuary in churches, hospitals, diplomatic missions and

---

[205] BBC 2003a.
[206] Olonisakin: 183, in: Adebajo/Rashid 2004.
[207] Reno 1998: 79.
[208] ibid.
[209] Jeffrey Goldberg, "A War Without Purpose in a Country Without Identity", New York Times Magazine, 22 January 1995, cit. in: Reno 1998: 79.

under Red Cross protection"[210]. Combatants of all warring factions committed horrific atrocities against innocent civilians such as the disembowelment and rape of women, hacking of people's limbs, torture and summary execution of civilians. Apart from the recruitment of children as soldiers to serve directly at the war front, fighters of the factions used children as spies, labourers, sex slaves or "wives" of commanders and cooks. Recalcitrance or disobeyance of orders led to the severe punishment and brutalization of these children. Exposed to brutality and adversity, Liberia's youth was emotionally and mentally traumatized and, to a considerable extent, criminalized by its experience of violence.[211] The population was uprooted in every sense as the fighting caused a high degree of disintegration of civilian communities and displacement of the Liberian population, thus disrupting the then existing social order. According to Alao et al., "By 1993, 700,000 Liberian refugees were living in the neighbouring states of Côte d'Ivoire, Ghana, Guinea, Nigeria, and Sierra Leone", more than 700,000 were estimated to have been internally displaced, and, by April 1994, about 1.4 million were receiving humanitarian assistance.[212]

Figure 4.6 Dire conditions at refugee camps around Monrovia, 2002[213]

---

[210] Communiqué of the ECOWAS Standing Mediation Committee, 7 August 1990, in: Weller 1994: 73.
[211] Olonisakin: 247-151, in: Adebajo/Rashid 2004.
[212] Alao et al. 1999: 48; cf. Olonisakin: 247-151, in: Adebajo/Rashid 2004.
[213] BBC 2002.

The battles between the warring factions were rarer than the violence directed against the civilian population. The warring factions' access to various economic resources meant that they did not have to rely on the local population for their sole support base. Consequently, the insurgents did not need to cultivate legitimacy among the local population.[214] The control of the civilian population by the warring factions depended on the stoking of continuous fear and insecurity and the use of ethnicity to fuel hatred towards Liberians of tribes, accused of supporting rival warring factions. Lack of social, military, and political discipline among the factions, moreover, heightened their propensity toward atrocities. The soldiers were mostly unpaid by the factions and basically lived off the communities they conquered.[215] Alao et al. attribute the instability within the factions to, first, the wide disparities in age, experience and motivation within the different sub-units of the individual factions; secondly, the frequent dispersion and reformation of smaller sub-units within a faction, thus causing command structures to be more ad hoc and fragile; and, thirdly, the inability of the faction leaders to control combatants below field commander's level, whose immediate concerns were local issues and survival needs. As the overall threat to a faction decreased (essentially, during peace negotiations), cohesion reduced, combatants beginning to "search for food, gainful employment, or opportunities for looting"[216]. The pursuit or protection of economic activities also further affected the command and control of combatants, affecting a group's cohesion and making conflict resolution more difficult.[217] For example, Roosevelt Johnson was suspended as faction leader of ULIMO-J in March 1996 as disputes with ULIMO-J fighters on diamond mining profits in Bomi County had weakened his position, exacerbated by the deployment of a new, non-compromising ECOMOG commander, who refused to collaborate in illicit mining operations.[218]

---

[214] Alao et al. 1999: 22f.

[215] ibid: 45ff.

[216] ibid.

[217] Cf. Cater: 31, in: Ballentine/Sherman 2003.

[218] Reno 1998: 104f.

Figure 4.7 Civilians fleeing the fight, 2003[219]

According to David Keen, "Increasingly, civil wars that appear to have begun with political aims have mutated into conflicts in which short-term economic benefits are paramount."[220] Civil wars can be fought for different reasons, with one reason being more important than another during a certain point in the conflict.

---

[219] BBC 2003d, 2009a.
[220] Cater: 29, in: Ballentine/Sherman 2003.

The motive of warfare was initially the deposition of the incumbent regime: "The express purpose of the group [NPFL] was to topple the regime of Samuel Doe."[221] Tom Woewiyu (NPFL) emphasized in June 1990 that the key to his party's demands was the resignation of Doe, "the source of all problems in Liberia ... the moment Mr Doe gets off our backs, the war would end".[222] On 27 July 1990, Charles Taylor, "the leader and President of the National Patriotic Front of Liberia", announced on Radio ELWA (Monrovia) that the Doe government was "dissolved" and "replaced by the government of the National Patriotic Reconstruction Assembly under my leadership" and announced elections "within six months".[223] Immediately following the assassination of Doe (9 September 1990), Charles Taylor (NPFL), Prince Johnson (INPFL), David Nimley (deputy commander of the AFL) as well as Harry Moniba (Doe's former vice president), all declared to be president of Liberia.[224] The civil war continued beyond Doe's deposition and death, although the initial political motive of warfare had been accomplished in principle. "It's the people who must decide on the future of Liberia, not Charles Taylor, not the NPFL", stated Taylor after he had just signed the Bamako cease-fire agreement on 28 November 1990; however, insisting that "no group has been recognised as the Interim Government"[225]. And further reiterated that, "we must respect what they have to say, because we are their servants".[226] Despite repeatedly phrasing that he only does what the Liberian people want him to do, Taylor used the NPFL as a vehicle for his political ambitions, eliminating potential rivals to his agenda within the NPFL ranks, not accepting any civilian interim administrations instituted after Doe's assassination and reneging on several peace agreements.[227] None of the factions provided "any coherent plan for fundamentally changing Liberia's political and economic structures and society": their motive for waging war was "based more on

---

[221] Adebajo 2002b: 42; cf. Reno 1998: 92f.
[222] BBC Monitoring Report, 14 June 1990, in: Weller 1994: 42.
[223] BBC Monitoring Report, 30 July 1990, in: Weller 1994: 62.
[224] Levitt 2005: 208; BBC Monitoring Report, 11 September 1990, in: Weller 1994: 97.
[225] BBC Monitoring Report, 30 November 1990, in: Weller 1994: 120.
[226] BBC Monitoring Report, 1 December 1990, in: Weller 1994: 121.
[227] Levitt 2005: 208; BBC Monitoring Report, 11 September 1990, in: Weller 1994: 97.

personal expediency than political ideology".[228] According to Adebajo, "Anti-NPFL factions claimed to be fighting for the democratic rights of all Liberians, but were essentially ad hoc ethnic armies led by individuals with dubious democratic credentials"[229]. For example, the United Liberation Movement of Liberia for Democracy (ULIMO) described itself as "a non-tribal and non-sectarian organisation born out of the desire of displaced Liberians to return home and continue their search for democratic freedom", aiming "to free Liberia "from the plunder of Charles Taylor"".[230]

Economic considerations only later became a more salient dimension of the Liberian conflict: Liberia's abundant economic resources provided the warring factions with the means to enrich themselves and continue to finance their war activities, thus adding an additional motive to warfare – natural resource exploitation. Battles were often fought for the control of natural resources-rich areas (such as Tubmanburg, Tapeta and Bomi County), abundant with diamonds, gold, timber, rubber and/or iron ore[231], as well as export routes and trade-significant locations. The port in Buchanan, for example, was a key NPFL-controlled asset for its trade in natural resources as well as import point of arms.[232] Hutchful and Aning argue that "there was a particularly opportunistic and instrumental edge to the manner in which Liberia's war was fought", owing to the "relative success and innovativeness with which faction groups exploited natural resources and negotiated economic deals with European, North American, and Asian firms".[233] By March 1991, the rapidly expanding political economy of the war involved thousands of people who consequently had an interest in the continuation of the conflict. The political motive became important again during peace negotiations, relating to the extent of inclusion of the warring factions in the transition government (membership of the Council of the State, distribution of ministerial positions, etc.),

---

[228] Adebajo 2002a: 47f.
[229] ibid.
[230] Adebajo 2002b: 91.
[231] Adebajo 2002a: 47f.
[232] Hutchful/Aning: 209, in: Adebajo/Rashid 2004.
[233] ibid: 210.

and the electoral contest for the presidential office. Ethnicity only played a role in that it was used instrumentally by the different leaders, first, as a means of repressing opposition under Doe and, secondly, as an instrument for recruitment by faction leaders.[234] The various factions claimed that their armies were formed for the defence of their own ethnic groups against attacks from other factions. Ethnicity, however, was only deployed to mask the personal aspirations of faction leaders.[235] Liberia's conflict thus includes political as well as economic motivations for warfare with varying importance during the lifeline of the conflict, whilst grievances under the Doe regime contributed to the initial popularity of the rebellion and high throng of recruits enjoyed by the NPFL.

The financing of the war thus became an important aspect of warfare itself, undermining prospects for peace as it contributed to the failure of implementing thirteen peace agreements between 1990 and 1996. The control and access to natural resources furthermore contributed to the proliferation of factions.[236] The various factions financed their war activities through looting, the sale of concession rights, the trade in natural resources, external assistance and the diversion of humanitarian aid. "Charles Taylor's NPFL was able to exploit the country's resources, while simultaneously having access to strategic communication lines," note Hutchful and Aning. By March 1991, the NPFL had established a lucrative export business based on diamonds, timber, iron ore, and gold with French, Belgian, Turkish, and Taiwanese firms.[237] According to Adebajo, "Taylor derived an estimated U.S.$75 million annually from these exports [diamonds, gold, timber, rubber and iron ore], [...] and an estimated U.S.$300,000 a month from foreign timber firms".[238] United Liberation Movement of Liberia for Democracy-K (ULIMO-K) sought to restore the Mandingoes' diamond trading links with Sierra Leone, which were broken off due to the control of Sierra Leone's diamond mining fields by the NPFL and

---

[234] Cf. Hutchful/Aning: 208, in: Adebajo/Rashid 2004.
[235] Cf. ibid: 209.
[236] ibid: 209f.
[237] ibid.
[238] Adebajo 2002a: 48.

dissident Sierra Leoneans in mid-1991. United Liberation Movement of Liberia for Democracy-J (ULIMO-J) controlled diamond mining in Bomi County, while the Liberia Peace Council (LPC) was involved in the exportation of rubber from the port of Buchanan. In 1995 alone, Liberia's warlords exported between U.S. $300 million and U.S. $500 million worth of diamonds and gold, U.S. $53 million worth of timber, and U.S. $27 million worth of rubber to markets in Europe and Southeast Asia.[239] Diversion of humanitarian aid and looting was also a phenomenon throughout the Liberian conflict.[240]

The financing aspect of the Liberian conflict had diverse dimensions but the illegal trade in natural resources was by far the most beneficial source of income for the warring factions. The warring factions were thus reliant on external linkages for the sustenance of their war fighting. If only it had been intended to protect their fixed assets and upkeep of operations, some larger foreign firms from the Doe period went into business arrangements with warring factions controlling their respective concession areas with varying degrees of collaboration. Charles Taylor, for example, struck a deal with Firestone Tire and Rubber Company. His security forces controlled workers on the plantation and used Firestone's marketing connections for the international sale of rubber whilst Firestone allegedly provided communications facilities to the NPFL and a supply base for military operations. A consortium of European community, U.S., and Japanese steel producers, planning to open a new mine astride the Liberia-Guinea border, paid Charles Taylor $10 million a month for the release of iron ore at the Liberian portion of the project, which was by late 1990 in the hands of the NPFL.[241] Moreover, Liberian warring parties forged collaborations with criminal networks to trade illegally acquired goods for the financing of their war activities. For example, the head of the Ukrainian Mafia, Leonid Minin, secured logging concessions for his company, Exotic and Tropical Timber Enterprise and, in turn, supplied Taylor, then Liberian head of

---

[239] Adebajo 2002a: 48.
[240] ibid: 50.
[241] Reno 1998: 100.

state, with arms, in contravention of a United Nations arms embargo.[242]

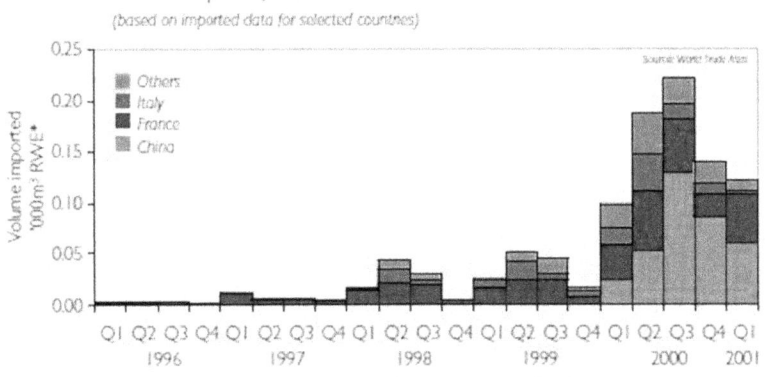

Figure 4.8   Timber imports from Liberia, 1996-2001[243]

The intensified linkages to players in the region and globally encompass the political, military and financial levels: at the political level, Liberia's warlords maintained personal relationships with other state leaders. Charles Taylor had close ties to the leaders of Libya, Burkina Faso and La Côte d'Ivoire, who supported his attempt at ousting Samuel Doe from power for their own personal reasons.[244] Furthermore, Liberia's civil war did not only affect the state, territory and people of Liberia but also had security implications for the neighbouring states Sierra Leone, Guinea and La Côte d'Ivoire. The influx of refugees, illegal transborder trade, the proliferation of small arms and light weapons (SALW), the extraction of easily accessible natural resources and support of dissidents by Liberian by warring factions weakened security structures along the borders of neighbouring states. The consequential spill-over led "atrocious civil wars in Sierra Leone, and Côte d'Ivoire, and the intermittent instability in Guinea's south-eastern region"[245].

---

[242] Global Witness 2002b: 16.
[243] Global Witness 2001d: 15. Figure 4.8 highlights the increased amount of timber exported during Taylor's regime.
[244] Adebajo 2002a: 48; Abdullah/Rashid: 181f., in: Adebajo/Rashid 2004.
[245] Aboagye/Bah 2005: 281.

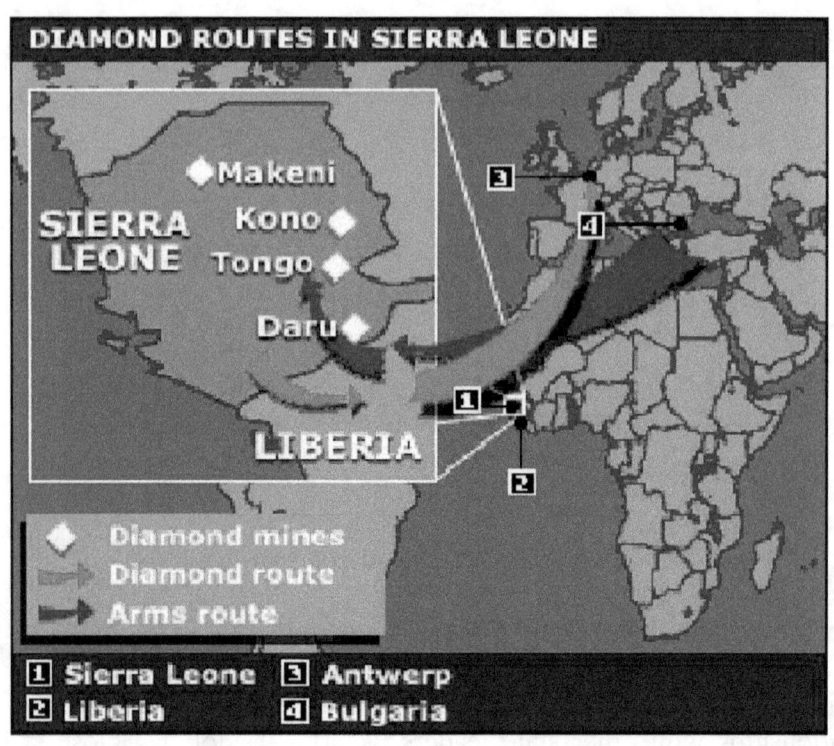

Map 4.2   Transnational diamond and arms routes[246]

West Africa saw the emergence of a complex regional conflict system and transnational orders of violence in areas of limited or failed statehood with immediate border areas mostly affected by conflict-related activities. Due to strategic and economic interests of warlords like Charles Taylor, warfare shifted from the political control of the capital to the politico-economical control of strategically important natural resources and trade routes, encompassing Liberian as well as neighbouring countries' territories (Map 4.2). By late 1990, the NPFL had established control over the cross-border trade between Sierra Leone and Liberia in diamonds, gold and agricultural products. Taylor had become France's third largest supplier of tropical hardwoods by 1991, which were transported via Gbarnga in Liberia to the ports

---

[246] BBC 2000.

of San Pedro and Abidjan, from where they would be shipped to international locations.[247]

Figure 4.9   Illicit diamond mining in Sierra Leone[248]

However, Taylor was not the only one who maintained transnational commerce and alliances. Alhaji Kromah organized Malinké-speaking people from the south of the Guinea-Liberia border with the purpose of recruiting fighters as well as forming commercial and military alliances with Malinkés on the Guinean side of the border. ULIMO supporters mined diamonds on both sides of the border which diverted revenues away from the Guinean state as well as from the NPFL. ULIMO's economic collaboration with old networks further widened factional splits

---

[247] Pugh/Cooper 2004: 91-110.
[248] Global Witness 2005d: 34.

in Guinea as it provided these partners with new trade opportunities without approval from President Lansana Conté. In February 1996, Conté faced a coup attempt by General Gbagbo Zoumanigui with the support of Malinké officers and entrepreneurs with ULIMO links.[249]

Peace Implementation Phase I: Cotonou Agreement (1993)

On 24 December 1989, NPFL fighters, led by Charles Taylor, crossed into Liberia's Nimba County from the Ivory Coast. The rebels rallied support among Nimba citizens, who had been affected by Doe's retaliation against Gios and Manos.[250] As the 12,500-strong NPFL was approaching Monrovia in May 1990, a summit of the West African subregional organization ECOWAS (Economic Community of West African States) established a five-member Standing Mediation Committee (SMC) with a mandate to mediate the Liberian civil war.[251] Peace talks in Freetown in June and July 1990 failed due to the NPFL's insistence on the resignation of Doe before the acceptance of any peace proposal. The August 1990 meeting of ECOWAS's SMC produced a peace plan to establish a peacekeeping force – Economic Community of West African States Cease-Fire Monitoring Group (ECOMOG) – with the mandate to supervise a cease fire and, following Doe's resignation, to establish an interim government (excluding the faction leaders) and organize elections after twelve months. When ECOMOG arrived in Monrovia on 24 August 1990, the Liberian state had collapsed[252], the warring factions proliferated in number, and the strongest faction, the NPFL, was against the intervention of ECOMOG because of Doe's close alliance with Nigeria's leader General Ibrahim Babangida[253]. ECOMOG's peacekeepers came under

---

[249] Reno 1998: 103.
[250] Kamara 2002: 15; Adebajo 2002a: 46; Alao et al. 1999: 20.
[251] Adebajo 2002a: 51ff.
[252] Levitt 2005: 206f.; Adebajo 2002a: 66f.
[253] Alao et al. 1999: 34.

immediate fire from the NPFL. Consequently, within a month, ECOMOG received 3,000 more troops, changed its mandate from peacekeeping to peace enforcement and was to establish a buffer zone around Monrovia. ECOMOG expelled the NPFL from the capital but compromised its neutrality by fighting alongside the anti-NPFL factions INPFL (Independent National Patriotic Front of Liberia) and the AFL (Armed Forces of Liberia); and later the United Liberation Movement of Liberia for Democracy (ULIMO).[254]

Several peace agreements had failed before the Cotonou Agreement of July 1993. The preceding Yamoussoukro IV Accord of 1991 collapsed after the NPFL launched a massive attack on ECOMOG' positions in Monrovia ('Operation Octopus') in October 1992. The peace process lay dormant until renewed ECOWAS and UN negotiations in Geneva and Cotonou brought about the Cotonou Agreement. Adebajo assigns the signing of the Cotonou Agreement on 25 July 1993 to the military operations launched by ECOMOG in early 1993: "ECOMOG had in effect bombed Charles Taylor to the negotiating table".[255] ECOMOG captured several strategic NPFL assets such as the Firestone rubber plantation near Harbel, Robertsfield International Airport and the Bassa highway leading from Monrovia to Buchanan. By the end of February 1993, ULIMO, furthermore, had gained control of virtually all of Northwestern Liberia. The growing military losses thus forced Taylor to the negotiating table. The Cotonou Agreement was in essence an expanded, revised version of the Yamoussoukro IV Accord of 1991 and, in turn, formed the basis for subsequent agreements in Akosombo, Accra and Abuja. It was signed by the incumbent interim government (IGNU), the warring factions ULIMO and NPFL. The 19 articles covered mechanisms for the monitoring of the ceasefire, the conducting of encampment, disarmament and demobilization of combatants, the establishment of a transitional government (LNTG) and an executive Council of State, election modalities, repatriation of refugees and displaced persons, and a general amnesty.[256] With

---

[254] Adebajo 2002a: 66f.
[255] Adebajo 2002b: 127.
[256] Sesay: 22, in: Accord 1996.

Cotonou, the peace process began to focus more specifically on the interests of the factions as a transitional power-sharing regime was instituted involving representatives of the factions, which set off the process of reducing the role of civilians in peace negotiations and Liberian politics. Moreover, ECOMOG's role in the implementation of the peace agreement was recast: Cotonou stipulated the expansion of ECOMOG with the addition of troops from ECOWAS states and from outside the West African sub-region and reduced ECOMOG's sole responsibility in implementing the peace agreement by the setting up of a United Nations Observer Mission (UNOMIL).[257]

Independent Variables

Figure 4.10   Diamonds in alluvial deposits[258]

---

[257] Alao: 36, in: Accord 1996; Alao et al. 1999: 42f.
[258] Global Witness 2005d: 36.

Figure 4.11   Camp of ex-LURD pit-sawyers, September 2005[259]

"Richly endowed with water, mineral resources, forests and a climate favourable to agriculture"[260], Liberia's economy has been highly dependent on the export of commodities such as timber, rubber, iron ore, gold and diamonds. Since 1951, Liberia has been among the leading producers of iron ore in Africa and one of the principal exporters of iron ore in the world. The largest deposits of iron ore can be found in the Bomi Hills, the Bong Range, the Mano Hills and Mount Nimba.[261] Gold in Liberia is almost entirely mined from alluvial deposits. Gold has been recovered in numerous river and stream deposits throughout Liberia, making placer mining widespread. Mine output varies greatly with many small deposits rapidly being exhausted.[262] Diamonds - both gem quality and industrial diamonds - have been found in alluvial deposits in different parts of the country with major locations in Lofa and Nimba Counties (Figure 4.10).

---

[259] Global Witness 2005d: 29.
[260] Hadden 2006: 11.
[261] ibid: 9f.
[262] ibid: 8f.

Liberia has, furthermore, been a producer and exporter of raw timber and rubber, apart from the production of coffee, cocoa, rice and cassava, and fishing along the coastal areas. Rubber was the most important cash crop before the civil war, generating the second-largest revenues after iron ore. The rubber estates were largely sustained by foreign investment, partly maintained during the conflict.[263] Additionally, Liberia maintains the last remaining extensive areas of thick tropical forest in West Africa, which measured some 4.5 million hectares in 1995.[264] However, between 1990 and 1995, some 134,000 hectares of forest were destroyed, and extensive logging operations from the late 1990s to 2003 highly fragmented the Cestos-to-Sapo corridor in Southeastern Liberia.[265] Maps 4.3, 4.4 and 4.5 depict surveys of Liberia's mineral resources and forestry, highlighting the widely dispersed distribution of resources throughout Liberia and the reduction of rainforest.

---

[263] Alao et al. 1999: 49f.
[264] Greenpeace 2001: 7.
[265] Sambolah 2005: 7f.

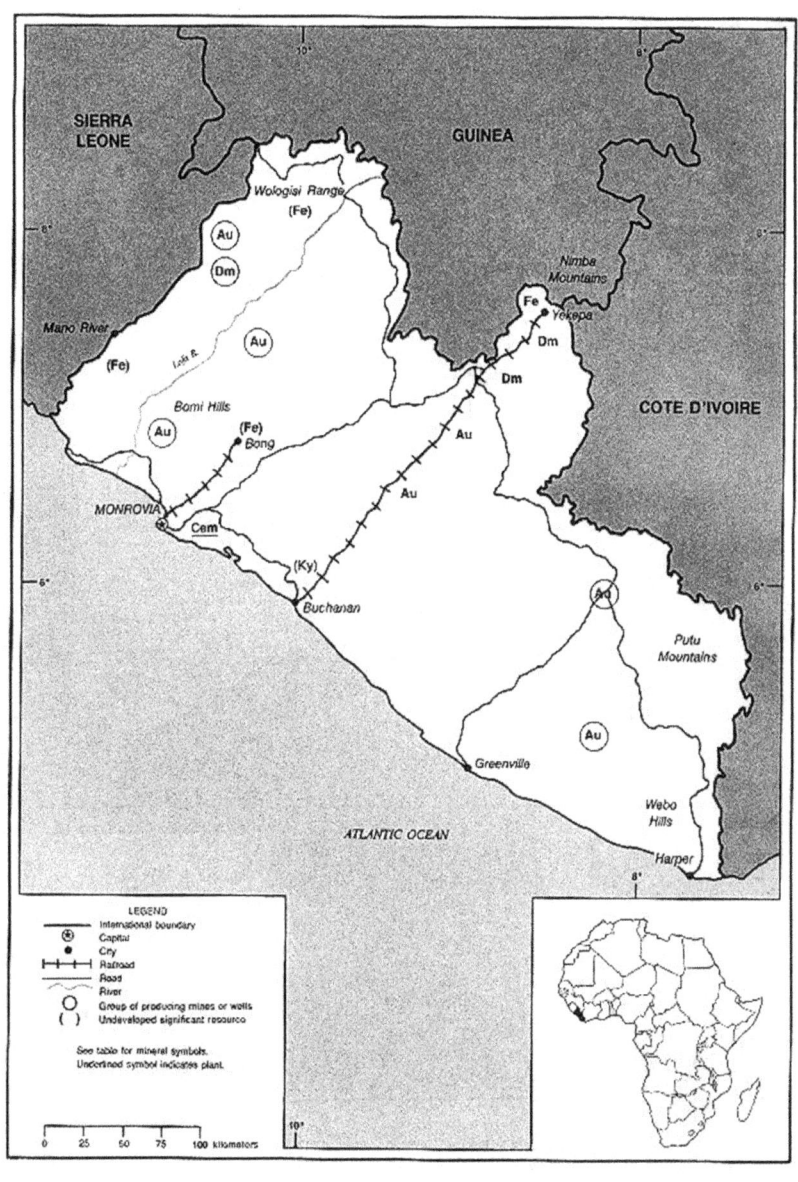

Map 4.3   Distribution of mineral resources in Liberia[266]

---

[266] USGS Minerals Information.

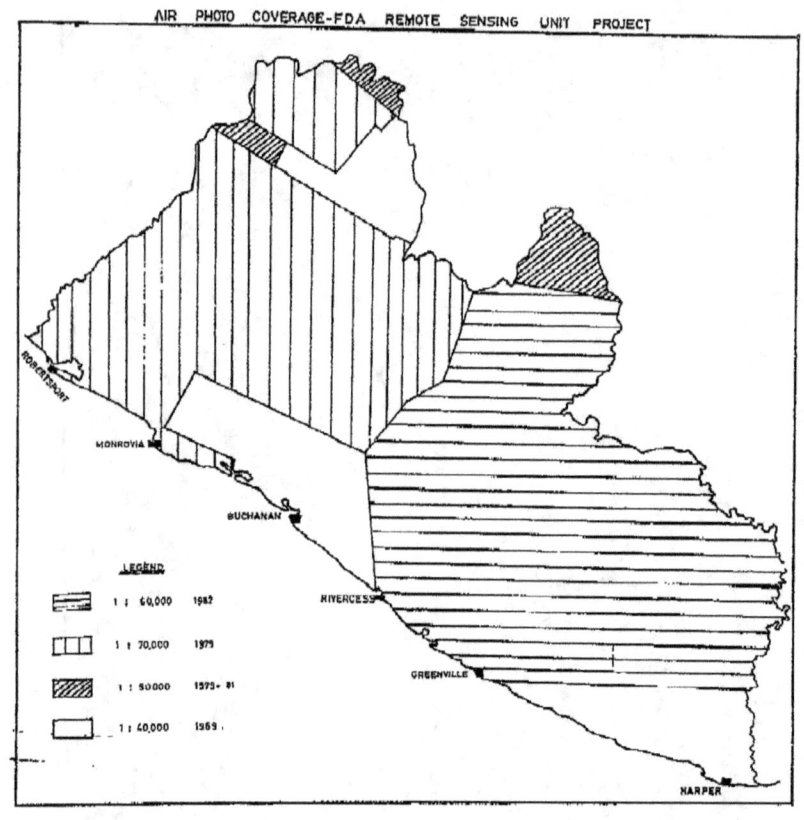

Map 4.4   Distribution of forestry in Liberia, 1969-1982[267]

---

[267] Hammermaster 1985: 13.

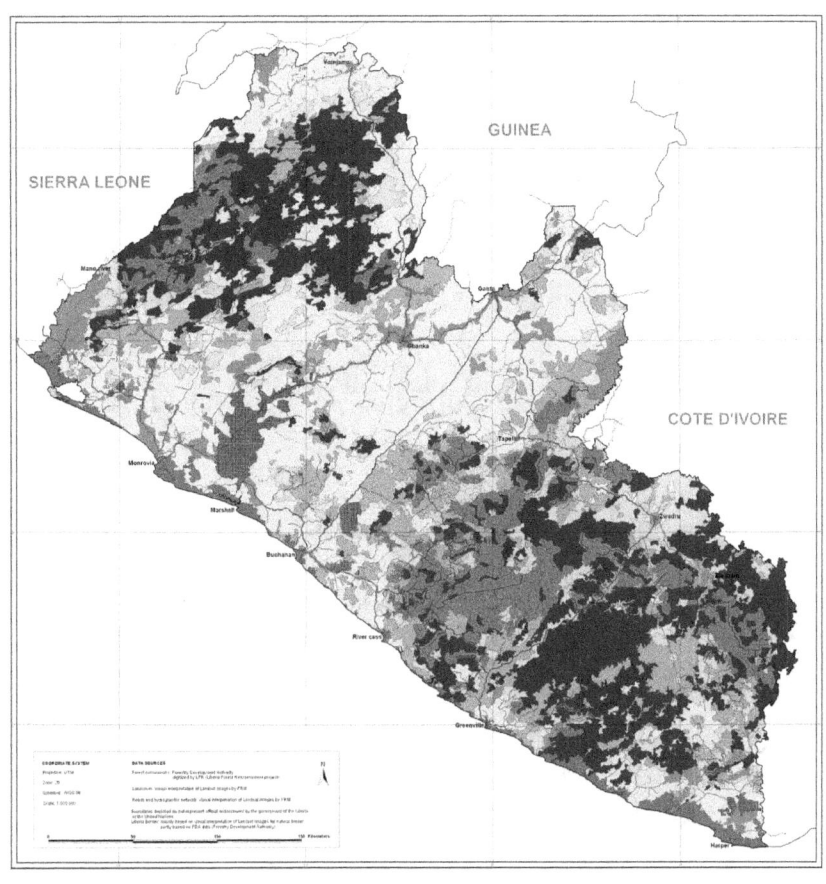

Map 4.5   Distribution of forestry in Liberia, 2004[268]

Liberia thus has an abundant wealth of resources, which can be classified as overwhelmingly lootable and difficult to obstruct (Table 4.1). Lootable resources – defined in respect to the ease of resource extraction – with their location in the hinterland were easily accessible for rebels for the financing of war activities. Timber, alluvial diamonds and gold can be found throughout Liberia and thus are classified as diffuse, widely available resources, which are difficult to obstruct by a government or regulating body. In comparison, point resources are highly concentrated such as Liberian iron ore mines, which require machinery for extraction, and are unlootable: the rebels still

---

[268] Bayol/Chevalier 2004.

benefited through the receiving of rents from existing mining companies and interested investors. The lootable classification of Liberia's resources implies that the valuable natural resources could be easily explored, mined and transported with a high price-to-weight ratio – especially with regard to diamonds – and thus presented an incentive for rebel groups to continue the warfare.[269] In respect to the presence of valuable natural resources, their easy exploitability and moderate obstructability to unobstructability, and the geographic dispersal of most of Liberia's natural resources, the dimension "valuable natural resources" can be classified as "difficult" for the whole timeline of the Liberian conflict.

Table 4.1 Classification of Liberia's Resources[270]		
	LOOTABLE	UNLOOTABLE
MODERATELY OBSTRUCTABLE	**Agricultural products Timber**	**Deep-shaft minerals**
UNOBSTRUCTABLE	**Alluvial gems**	-

At the signing of the Cotonou Agreement, three main factional areas were in existence, respectively controlled by the AFL in cooperation with ECOMOG, ULIMO, and the NPFL.[271] The AFL was the remnant of Doe's army, with many of its members either joining or collaborating with ULIMO and the emerging LPC. During the NPFL offensive in late 1992, the AFL was re-activated, having been confined to barracks in November 1990.[272] Controlling up to 95 percent of the country in 1990, the NPFL's control of Liberian territory drastically reduced with the emergence of new factions and the expansion of ECOMOG's controlled territory. The Independent National Patriotic Front of Liberia (INPFL), a breakaway faction of the NPFL led by Prince Yormie Johnson, dissolved in late 1992 after its role in the

---

[269] Cf. Lujala 2003.
[270] Ross: 49, 55, in: Ballentine/Sherman 2003.
[271] Alao et al. 1999: 45.
[272] Accord 1996: 82; Adebajo 2002a: 47.

conflict had declined.[273] ULIMO was formed in May 1991 by former AFL fighters and Krahn and Mandingo politicians in Sierra Leone and entered Western Liberia in September 1991.[274] By the end of 1992, ULIMO had gained control of about 20 percent of Liberian territory, capturing most of Northwestern Liberia.[275] As OAU Envoy Reverend Banana noted, "Previous agreements took place when the NPFL was in a much stronger position. But now the balance of forces has changed and, given this reality on the ground, one hopes that it will cooperate in the completion of the peace agreement"[276]. The change in distribution of power thus was a favourable condition for the rekindling of the peace process as the NPFL had lost its then high bargaining power. Hence, the dimension "distribution of power" can be classified as "easy" because none of the factions maintained more than 50% of Liberia's territory. The value of the dimension "number of conflict parties", on the contrary, is "difficult" as more than two parties were present at the time of Cotonou.

The Uppsala Conflict Data Program counts 25 battle-related deaths for the year 1993, while war-related deaths account to "under 2000" for the same year.[277] However, the resumption of fighting in late 1992 continued into 2003: in January 1993, ECOMOG launched a ten-day offensive. In the following months, ECOMOG was engaging Taylor in "a long, bloody march toward Gbarnga"[278]. Battles between ULIMO and the NPFL, and counter-attacks by the NPFL on ECOMOG's positions also characterized early 1993.[279] The number of 25 battle-related deaths thus does not represent actual numbers. War-related deaths are also estimated as too low: nearly 300 Liberians were killed and more than 700 wounded in the Harbel area massacre of civilians alone on 6 June 1993.[280] Due to the extensive battles throughout 1993 between ECOMOG and the

---

[273] Accord 1996: 82; Adebajo 2002a: 46; Alao et al. 1999: 41. The INPFL had been responsible for the murder of President Samuel Doe in September 1990.
[274] Accord 1996: 82; Adebajo 2002a: 47.
[275] Adebajo 2002a: 55.
[276] PANA, Lagos, 23 July 1993, cited in: Weller 1994: 339; cf. Adebajo 2002b: 127.
[277] Uppsala Conflict Data Program 2008: Liberia, War & Minor Conflict 1993.
[278] Adebajo 2002b: 121.
[279] Adebajo 2002b: 122; United Nations, S/25402, 12 March 1993, in: Weller 1994: 282.
[280] United Nations, S/25919, 9 June 1993, in: Weller 1994: 300.

NPFL, and ULIMO and the NPFL, the dimension "casualties (combatants and civilians)" is classified as "difficult".

ECOWAS member states, to varying degrees, contributed troops to ECOMOG and were involved in peace mediation efforts. Contrary to these developments, some ECOWAS member states directly supported Liberian conflict parties with financial and/or military means. Both Burkina Faso and Libya provided NPFL combatants with training in guerrilla warfare in Libyan and Burkinabè military camps. Burkina Faso remained the main source for arms supplies to the NPFL throughout Liberia's civil war, and 700 soldiers of the Burkinabè army assisted Taylor at the initial invasion.[281] In return, Compaoré benefited from trade ties to the NPFL leader. La Côte d'Ivoire was a major conduit for Taylor's arms and supplies, and Ivorian-based commercial interests benefited from NPFL mineral and timber concessions.[282] Initially opposed to the deployment of ECOMOG, La Côte d'Ivoire became increasingly involved in the ECOWAS diplomatic process by mid-1991 and was a leading force in the securing of the four Yamoussoukro Accords.[283] In late 1992, La Côte d'Ivoire began to distance itself from the NPFL, expressing concern over the destabilizing effects of the Liberian civil war on its territory, sending 500 troops to guard its border with Liberia.[284] When the war was taken to Sierra Leone in March 1991 by NPFL-aligned combatants, Sierra Leone's national security became inextricably tied to its support for ECOMOG. In July 1990, NPFL guerrillas launched a brief incursion into Guinea, which led Guinea's General Lansana Conté to threaten the launch of a unilateral intervention into Liberia.[285] Several failed peace agreements, continued NPFL aggression, and Nigerian fears of francophone-NPFL collaboration, led elements within ECOMOG to provide covert support to ULIMO.[286] ECOMOG's changed strategy of peace enforcement in late 1992 led to a close cooperation between ECOMOG and the AFL and

---

[281] Adebajo 2002b: 122
[282] Adebajo 2002b: 54f.; Accord 1996: 87f.
[283] Accord 1996: 87f.
[284] Adebajo 2002b: 105f.
[285] ibid: 62.
[286] Alao: 35f., in: Accord 1996; Accord 1996: 83.

ULIMO factions.[287] ECOMOG officers supplied ULIMO with arms, intelligence and uniforms, and after "Operation Octopus" ECOMOG openly allied with ULIMO and re-armed the AFL for their combined bombing of NPFL-held areas.[288] Liberia's factions thus were financially and/or militarily supported by neighbouring states; the dimension "neighbouring states" taking the value "difficult". The ECOWAS states were not united in a common strategy for Liberia, thus contributing to spoiler behaviour of factions. As more than three dimensions were set as difficult, the variable "nature of the conflict" is rated as "difficult" for peace implementation phase II.

The Cotonou Agreement was the most comprehensive Liberian peace agreement theretofore, including the sub-goals demobilization, disarmament, power sharing and elections among the list of to be executed tasks. ECOMOG, in its expanded form, and UNOMIL were to supervise and monitor the implementation of the Agreement (Article 3).[289] ECOMOG was to provide the necessary security in creating buffer zones, seal the borders "to prevent cross-border attacks, infiltration or importation of arms"[290] and to monitor all points of entry. The parties were to disarm to ECOMOG and commit their combatants to encampment centres set up by ECOMOG, monitored and verified by UNOMIL.[291] Demobilization of Article 9 was less specific about the planned process, calling upon the United Nations and other financiers to programme and finance demobilization and reintegration of former combatants into society. ECOMOG's absolute authority assigned to it in previous agreements was downscaled by the constant emphasis in the Agreement on the monitoring and verification role of UNOMIL towards all specified implementation processes.[292] However, the Agreement failed to assign a "universally competent authority"[293] to coordinate the separate but related modalities of the peace

---

[287] Accord 1996: 88.
[288] ibid: 97.
[289] Alao et al. 1999: 133.
[290] ibid: 134.
[291] ibid: 136f.
[292] ibid: 43.
[293] ibid: 54.

process, involving different parties and organisations with separate command structures and agenda setting. Especially by its failure to address the "question of ECOMOG and UNOMIL's mutual security modalities, the Cotonou plan separated the coordinating element of the peace process, which was to be done by the UN, from responsibility for security and civil order, which rested with ECOMOG"[294].

The Liberia National Transitional Government (LNTG) was to have representatives of all parties to the conflict: the three parties to the Agreement – the Interim Government of National Unity of Liberia (IGNU), the NPFL, and ULIMO – assigned members to the established five-member Council of State (COS) and the judicial and legislative branches of the LNTG.[295] Cotonou thus gave a larger say and responsibilities to the warring factions in the transitional period. Most of the most important sub-goals were addressed in the Cotonou Agreement. However, the specifications lacked preciseness with regard to the execution of tasks and respective timelines: first, it left it to the LNTG to derive the particulars through processes of consultation, secondly, the schedules of implementation were to be drawn up afterwards by ECOMOG and UNOMIL, and, thirdly, the financial means for the different tasks had not been allocated. Furthermore, the expectations were too high about the capabilities of the LNTG as well as of ECOMOG and UNOMIL, which did not have the required strength and resources at the time of the Agreement. Under these preconditions, within a time span of six to seven months, the parties were expected to implement the tasks disarmament, demobilization, encampment, repatriation and elections. A ceasefire was to be established by 1 August 1993, the transitional government (LNTG) installed by the end of August 1993 and the holding of presidential elections set for February/March 1994.[296] Alao et al. consequently argue that "the time to achieve the necessary conditions for successful disarmament, rehabilitation and resettlement and to conduct an election was impossibly short"[297]. Furthermore, Article 16 stated

---

[294] Alao et al. 1999: 55.
[295] ibid: 52-61.
[296] Adebajo 2002a: 56; Alao et al. 1999: 41ff.
[297] Alao et al. 1999: 64.

that the "transitional Government shall have a life span of approximately six (6) months"[298]. The word "approximately" led to contradictory interpretations by the parties.[299] In the event of any occurring contentious issues, no fora or conflict resolution mechanisms were set up for their resolution. Acts of violations specified in the Agreement, such as the recruitment and training of combatants[300], were to be investigated by UNOMIL or a Violations Committee. In the event of non-compliance by the violating party, ECOMOG was authorized to "resort to the use of its peace-enforcement powers against the violator"[301]. The measurements against violators of the Agreement's provisions, however, were not specified, and violations only related to security issues. The dimension "sub-goals" is classified as "low": the tasks "demobilization" and "elections" were inadequately specified, and the sub-goals "reintegration", "trade in natural resources" and "reforms" were not addressed. "Future contentious issues" were not referred to in the agreement, taking the value "low". The dimensions "guarantees" and "included actors" are valued as "high" as security and power-sharing guarantees were provided for the transition period, and all parties to the conflict were included in the peace negotiations as well as the transitional government. Nonetheless, there was no stipulation in the Agreement about whether any guarantees were to hold beyond elections. "Schedules", "distribution of tasks" and "spoiler" have the classification "medium" due to their inadequate or problematic specification. As less than four dimensions had the value "high" and more than one "low", the variable "quality of the peace agreement design" with respect to the Cotonou Agreement is rated as "low".

---

[298] Alao et al. 1999: 57, 142.
[299] Cf. ibid: 57.
[300] ibid: 135.
[301] ibid: 138.

Compared to previous peace agreements, the Cotonou Agreement saw a greater participation of the United Nations. The United Nations had limited its involvement in the Liberian conflict to the condemnation of the war and rhetorical support for ECOWAS' peacekeeping efforts. ECOMOG now was to

Figure 4.12 West African peace-keepers[302]

implement the peace agreement in close association with UNOMIL. The practical involvement of the United Nations and the inclusion of OAU peacekeepers from Uganda and Tanzania in ECOMOG conferred some level of impartiality on ECOMOG, which had been compromised due to its military offensive against the NPFL in the aftermath of 'Operation Octopus'.[303] An advance team of 30 military observers was dispatched to Liberia on 6 August to gather information on the proposed establishment of UNOMIL.[304] ECOMOG worked out a detailed concept of operations covering the provisions of the Agreement and under which ECOMOG troops would be stationed at entry points, airports and seaports. ECOMOG divided Liberia into the sectors Eastern, Northern, Western and Greater Monrovia and was to station troops in all four sectors. To fulfil the requirements of the Agreement, ECOMOG planned to expand its forces by 4,000 troops to be deployed throughout the country.[305] However, it was not until October 1993 before it was announced which OAU countries were willing to contribute troops to ECOMOG.[306] Tanzanian troops began arriving in late December 1993, with troops from Uganda following in January 1994.[307] With the addition of troops from other ECOWAS member states and troops from outside the West African sub-region, ECOMOG

---

[302] CNN 1997d.

[303] Alao et al. 1999: 43.

[304] United Nations, S/26422, 9 September 1993, in: Weller 1994: 374.

[305] ibid: 376.

[306] Report, 10 October 1993, in: Weller 1994: 420.

[307] AFP News Agency, 24 December 1993, in: Weller 1994: 450.

reached a total of 11,500 troops.[308] UN Security Council resolution 866 (1993) established UNOMIL for a period of seven months, subject to the achievement of substantive progress in the implementation of Cotonou.[309] The first UN military observers arrived in Liberia in November 1993[310], and UNOMIL attained its total authorized strength of 368 military observers in early January 1994. Concerning the financing of to-be implemented tasks, disarmament and demobilization were to be covered by a Trust Fund for Liberia. However, as of 13 December 1993, no pledges had been made to the Trust Fund for this purpose.[311] By February 1994, $8.83 million had been contributed to the Trust Fund for the deployment and eventual repatriation of additional ECOMOG troops. However, the provision of stipends to the additional troops and the logistic and maintenance support required for their deployment throughout Liberia were not available.[312] Existing ECOMOG troop-contributing countries also faced difficulties in covering the costs for logistics of the peacekeeping force, and domestic pressures caused Nigeria to express its intention of withdrawing its contingent before 31 March 1994.[313] The logistical and financial shortfalls culminated in delayed deployment of UNOMIL staff and additional contingents for ECOMOG to Liberia, affecting the initiation of peace implementing processes. The dimensions "provided assistance", "resources", "mandate", "spoiler" and "commitment" can thus be valued as "medium" because the international commitment was in these respects not adequate. The value of the dimension "number of peacekeepers" is determined as "high": owing to the relative small size of Liberian territory and initial high interest of combatants to disarm, the eventually reached number of peacekeepers was adequate. The variable "international interest and commitment" can thus be classified as "medium" as most of the dimensions fall into the category "medium", with none taking the value "low".

---

[308] Adebajo 2002a: 57; Alao et al. 1999: 43, 62.
[309] United Nations, S/RES/866, 22 September 1993, in: Weller 1994: 413.
[310] AFP News Agency, 8 November 1993, in: Weller 1994: 426.
[311] United Nations, S/26868, 13 December 1993, in: Weller 1994: 443.
[312] United Nations, S/1994/168, 14 February 1994, in: Weller 1994: 458ff.; Adebajo 2002a: 57.
[313] AFP News Agency, 29 September 1993, in: Weller 1994: 416.

Action Theory

The capturing of strategic NPFL assets by ECOMOG and anti-NPFL warring factions reduced the NPFL's stream of income in the pre-Cotonou period, which in turn made the NPFL more accessible to renewed peace negotiations. The proliferation of factions also led to a significant loss of territory for the previously predominant faction NPFL. Consequently, for the NPFL, the continuance of warfare was tied to increased costs at the time of Cotonou. Considering the difficult nature of the conflict, the low quality of the peace agreement design and the medium international interest and commitment, the conditions for a successful peace implementation, however, were not ideal. Despite the pledge of security guarantees in the Cotonou Agreement, the regional peacekeepers and the observer mission did not have the resources to deploy throughout the country and to set up the number of anticipated encampment sites (Maps 4.6 and 4.7). The security of demobilized and disarmed ex-combatants thus could not be guaranteed for the whole territory of Liberia. Reintegration programmes which would have provided ex-combatants with an alternative to war activities were not included in the Agreement. The only option for combatants, despite their initial high interest in disarmament, was the resumption of war activities as no alternative was provided for their daily upkeep and future occupation. Benefits for peace implementation spelt out in the agreement were that representatives of all conflict parties were to be included in the transitional government. However, Article 16 of Cotonou prohibited members of the transitional government to run for the next general and presidential elections. Owing to the inadequate international commitment and interest and the guarantee of power-sharing only being applicable to the short transition period, the benefit of continued war activities was higher than the benefit of peace implementation. It was, moreover, beneficial for the NPFL that ECOMOG had stopped its military advances into NPFL-held territory in May 1993. The lull in fighting gave ample opportunity for the NPFL to regain strength, providing Taylor with "another breathing space to stall peace"[314]. The conflict

---

[314] Kamara 2002: 20.

parties, furthermore, continued to pursue their commercial and territorial interests unhindered. Hence, warfare and war-related activities such as the illegal trade in natural resources were, according to the warring factions, more favourable than peace as the necessary incentives and guarantees for peace implementation were not or inadequately provided. The costs of peace implementation outweighed the benefits derived from war activities. The warring factions thus preferred the course of action H2 Non-cooperation in peace implementation to H1 Cooperation in peace implementation.

ECOMOG DEPLOYMENT   MAP 2

Map 4.6   ECOMOG deployment, 1994[315]

[315] Alao/Mackinlay 1995: 28.

MAP 3

Map 4.7   UNOMIL deployment, 1994[316]

Dependent Variable

A deadlock between IGNU and NPFL soon reappeared after Cotonou: IGNU called for disarmament before it handed power to the new transitional government while the NPFL and ULIMO called for a new interim government before disarmament. Charles Taylor was unwilling to disarm to ECOMOG, warning that only the LNTG had the power to supervise disarmament, contrary to the Agreement's terms.[317] Representatives of the three signatories to the Agreement met in Cotonou on 3 November 1993 to resolve their differences and establish the new interim government. Having reached agreement on the members of the Council of State, legislature, elections commission, and Supreme Court, the meeting broke down over nominees for remaining cabinet posts.

---

[316] Alao/Mackinlay 1995: 29.
[317] Adebajo 2002b: 137.

On 15 February 1993, the three signatories of Cotonou signed the Monrovia agreement. It stipulated that three events were to occur simultaneously: the installation of the LNTG, disarmament and the deployment of ECOMOG and UNOMIL peacekeepers to all Liberian territory. [318] Hence, concomitant with the installation of the LNTG on 7 March 1994, ECOMOG and UNOMIL started deploying to the countryside, establishing three encampment and demobilisation centres for NPFL, AFL and ULIMO combatants, respectively. On the arrival of combatants at the sites, ECOMOG soldiers, with observance by UNOMIL military personnel, took and registered their weapons. After a brief interview, UNOMIL civilian staff issued identity cards to the demobilized combatants. The combatants underwent medical examination before receiving clothing, rations, agricultural tools and transport to a community of their choice. In the first month, 2,200 of the estimated 33,000 combatants were demobilized. But as fighting erupted again and political disagreements among the factions hampered peace implementation, disarmament came to a near standstill by June 1994, bringing the total number of disarmed combatants to only 3,612.[319] Locally arranged "food for work" programmes were successful in some communities but failed to spread into an area-wide trend that could have motivated more combatants to disarm. The focus on short-term emergency aid by relief agencies further discouraged long-term recovery plans, for example, the resumption of subsistence agriculture.[320] As of early April 1994, ambushes of ECOMOG soldiers by Liberia's factions forced ECOMOG to retreat its troops and UNOMIL to withdraw its observers to Monrovia, reducing its numbers from 368 to 90. Warnings by ECOMOG's Field Commander Marc Inienger of resorting to peace-enforcement actions went unheeded. ECOMOG was becoming a useful scapegoat for the factions in their attempts to resist disarmament as the various factions accused ECOMOG of lenience towards their opponents.[321] The lack of adequate international support also thwarted ECOMOG's peace-implementing efforts. The inclusion of UNOMIL

---

[318] Adebajo 2002b: 142f.
[319] Adebajo 2002a: 57; Adebajo 2002b: 137ff.; cf. Alao et al. 1999: 60f.
[320] Alao et al. 1999: 65-68.
[321] Adebajo 2002a: 57; Adebajo 2002b: 137ff.

peacekeepers did not lead to an improvement of ECOMOG's logistical shortcomings as the UN mission declined to share its resources and equipment with ECOMOG.[322] Other key areas of disagreement between ECOMOG and UNOMIL essentially related to the coordination of activities.[323]

Cotonou reflected the euphoric planning of the peace agreements, stipulating the completion of disarmament and elections within seven months. By May 1994, serious obstacles to an autumn election could be identified. Between 700,000 and 1.2 million Liberians were still displaced. The ad hoc Liberian Elections Commission had neither the "expertise nor the executive energy"[324] to deal with revisions of the electoral system by September 1994. The lack of executive energy, moreover, was emblematic for the LNTG: the five members of the Council of State disagreed over appointments to public corporations and autonomous agencies as the factions struggled for their share of Liberia's spoils. The LNTG was unable to extend its authority beyond Monrovia and remained dependent on foreign donors for its financial survival and income from Liberia's issuance of flags of convenience to foreign vessels.[325] With the factions maintaining their control of Liberian territory and the emergence of new as well as splinter factions, peace implementation became an impossible task. The two new factions, Liberia Peace Council (LPC) and Lofa Defence Force (LDF), that emerged by the end of 1993, had nothing to gain from the successful implementation of Cotonou.[326] LPC was fighting the NPFL in Sinoe and Rivercess Counties for the control of Southeastern Liberia. At the opposite side of the country, the LDF gained several towns in Lofa County from ULIMO. By early 1994, ULIMO had split into two factions – ULIMO-K led by Alhaji Kromah and ULIMO-J controlled by Roosevelt Johnson.[327] By the end of 1994, at least seven main factions vied for supremacy in Liberia (Map 4.8).[328] UN Secretary-General Boutros Boutros-Ghali described the

---

[322] Adebajo 2002b: 131f.
[323] ibid: 141.
[324] Alao et al. 1999: 67f.
[325] Adebajo 2002b: 142f.
[326] Adebajo 2002a: 56ff.; Adebajo 2002b: 129, 131.
[327] Adebajo 2002b: 136f.; Accord 1996: 82; Adebajo 2002a: 47.
[328] Adebajo 2002b: 140.

current military situation in Liberia in 1994 as "small-scale bush fighting. The results are not large military victories, but deaths mostly of civilians, the decimation of entire villages and the breakdown of any semblance of law and order"[329]. Even as representatives of factions were part of the LNTG, their fighters continued to battle each other for the control of the countryside. The implementation phase I thus can be classified as a "partial success" as less than four of the sub-goals of top priority were implemented: the dimensions "demobilization", "disarmament", "power sharing or political participation" were partly implemented, taking the value "medium". In comparison, "reintegration", "trade in natural resources" and "reforms" were not instituted, and "elections" did not take place due to the persistent political divisions in the LNTG and increased fighting in the countryside.

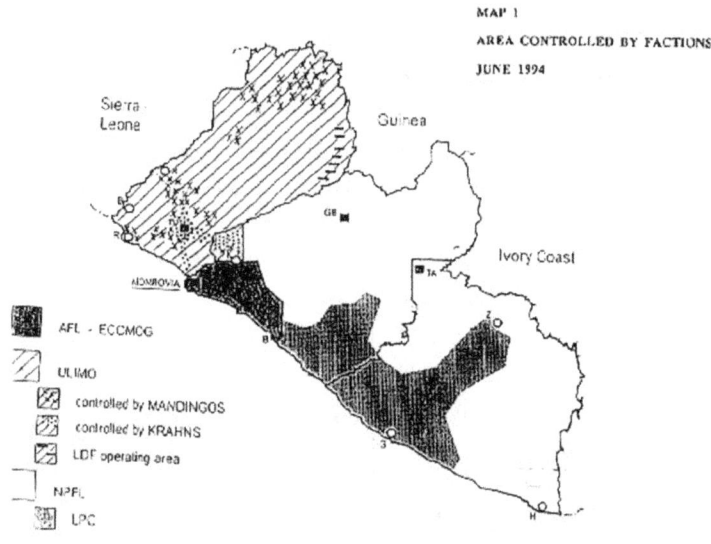

MAP 1

AREA CONTROLLED BY FACTIONS

JUNE 1994

Map 4.8   Areas controlled by Liberian factions, June 1994[330]

---

[329] Boutros-Ghali 1994, cited in: Adebajo 2002b: 140.
[330] Alao/Mackinlay 1995: 28.

Summary

The peace agreement of Cotonou was the most comprehensive agreement up to then. An important factor was the higher involvement of the United Nations in the peace implementation phase, thereby shouldering responsibilities together with the sub-regional peacekeeping force ECOMOG. Peace implementation had, however, shortcomings at several fronts: on the one hand, the high expectations toward ECOMOG, UNOMIL and the transitional government did not accord with the available resources and capabilities under the condition of a difficult conflict environment, and, on the other hand, the implementation phase presented a welcome breathing space for the conflict parties to rearm and reorganise. Aside the persisting difficulties to implement the peace formula disarmament – reintegration – elections, the emergence of two new warring factions, continuous violations of the agreed-upon cease fire and the rekindling of large scale hostilities between the conflict parties caused the peace process to completely break down. The lack of restrictions on the trade in natural resources also made continuous warfare possible as the warring factions continued to derive revenues from this sector. Modelled on Cotonou, the subsequent Akosombo and Accra agreements of 1994 increasingly gave more power to the conflict parties in the executive of the transitional government. However, they could not halt the factional disputes over government posts, nor did they significantly stem the violence in the hinterland as the conditions set down in the respective agreements were not met.[331]

Peace Implementation Phase II: Abuja I and II Agreement (1995/96)

In June 1995, arranged by ECOWAS chairman and Ghanaian president Jerry Rawlings, Charles Taylor spent four days with Nigerian leader General Sani Abacha in a rapprochement

---

[331] Adebajo 2002a: 56-58; Sesay: 23, in: Accord 1996.

between ECOMOG's dominant troop-contributing country and Liberia's strongest faction. The rapprochement was an important trust-building factor for the NPFL towards ECOWAS's intentions in renewed peace negotiations, helping to lay the groundwork for the signing of the Abuja Agreement on 19 August 1995.[332] During a meeting of ECOWAS leaders in Abuja in August 1995, Nigeria's foreign minister Tom Ikimi called for a Council of State that "could provide strong and effective leadership and would be able to control the whole territory of Liberia"[333]. One significant departure from previous agreements, consequently, was that the Abuja Agreement provided for all major warlords to be directly seated in the six-man Council of State. The council was chaired by Professor Wilton Sankawulo with equal vice-chairmanship for faction leaders Charles Taylor (NPFL), Alhaji Kromah (ULIMO-K), and George Boley (LPC-Coalition) and two civilian representatives. Abuja, furthermore, permitted the faction leaders to contest the presidential elections stipulated for August 1996. After six years of civil war, war-weariness among the 33,000 faction fighters led some of them to voluntarily disarm to ECOMOG even before the signing of the Agreement. Abuja raised great hopes in Liberia. Nonetheless, irreconcilable differences and personal ambitions of the warlords continued to plague the transitional government with discontent festering within groups who believed themselves sidelined in the settlement. Factions continued to guard their territorial and commercial resources, with ongoing violence between NPFL and LPC and between sub-groupings of ULIMO. Increasing numbers of combatants entered Monrovia with the increment of tensions, culminating in the eruption of violence in the capital on 6 April 1996. Following the factional violence, a second Abuja agreement was signed with the objective of correcting flaws of the first Abuja agreement.[334]

---

[332] Adebajo 2002a: 59f.; Sesay: 23, in: Accord 1996.
[333] Adebajo 2002a: 60.
[334] Adebajo 2002a: 60f.; Sesay: 23f., in: Accord 1996; Alao: 73, in: Accord 1996; Adebajo 2002b: 168f., 181f.

Independent Variables

The leaders of neighbouring states were tired of bearing the cost and disruption of the Liberian conflict which, with varying degrees, directly affected the stability of their own territory.[335] An increment of cross-border raids by Liberian combatants on Ivorian plantations and villages forced Ivorian leader Henry Konan Bédié to increase border security in the western region of his country. It was also an attempt to stem the flow of arms through its territory as Abidjan was becoming "an entrepôt for guns and drugs from Liberia, increasing the incidence of violent crime in Côte d'Ivoire"[336]. During the ECOWAS Committee of Nine Meeting in Abuja in August 1996, La Côte d'Ivoire was one of the major advocates for sanctions against Liberia's factions, urging Burkina Faso to discontinue military support to the NPFL. A month earlier, Abidjan had denied Taylor permission to fly over its airspace to travel to Nigeria.[337] Blaise Compaoré, the Burkinabè leader, was intimately involved in the negotiations that led to the rapprochement between the NPFL and Nigeria in 1995. As Nigeria made peace with Taylor and no longer supported anti-NPFL factions, Burkina Faso began to actively support ECOMOG. It was significant for subregional unity that four francophone members offered to contribute troops to ECOMOG, among them Burkina Faso and Côte d'Ivoire.[338] Consequently, ECOWAS states put pressure on client factions, threatening to withdraw their political support if the conflict parties did not halt their intransigence to peace. The dimension "neighbouring states", hence, is classified as "easy".

The proliferation of warring factions complicated peace negotiations as agreements had to be inclusive of and acceptable to an increasing number of interests. The collapse of the Yamoussoukro, Cotonou, and Akosombo agreements was also largely due to the emergence of new groups who had either been left out or refused to attend peace talks.[339] The LPC and LDF had been excluded from Akosombo, despite their control over parts of

---

[335] Alao et al. 1999: 119.
[336] Adebajo 2002b: 186f.
[337] ibid: 193-196.
[338] Adebajo 2002a: 66; Adebajo 2002b: 166, 193-196.
[339] Sesay: 76f., in: Accord 1996.

Southeastern and Northern Liberia, meaning that the Akosombo Agreement did not bear resemblance to military and political realities. The National Patriotic Front of Liberia – Central Revolutionary Council (NPFL-CRC) emerged as a breakaway group of the NPFL in September 1994 and formed a loose coalition with other anti-NPFL factions to expel the NPFL from Gbarnga. Compared with the three signatories of Akosombo, not less than eight groups signed the Accra Clarification and the subsequent Abuja Agreement.[340] The proliferation of factions led to the intensification of fighting in the countryside, engulfing more than 80 percent of the country by the end of 1994. In the first eight months of 1995, fighting continued between the NPFL and anti-NPFL factions, and between ULIMO-K and ULIMO-J, largely for the control of mineral-rich territories.[341] On 6 April 1996, police forces, enforced by NPFL and ULIMO-K fighters, attempted to arrest ULIMO-J's leader Roosevelt Johnson on charges of murder. Consequently, many fighters flooded into Monrovia, leading to the eruption of fierce fighting in the capital between NPFL and ULIMO-K forces, on the one hand, and ULIMO-J elements supported by the AFL and LPC, on the other.[342] The years 1995 and 1996 thus had a high conflict intensity: the Uppsala Conflict Data Program counts between 10,000 and 15,000 war-related deaths for the year 1995 alone.[343] It, however, does not record any intensity level for 1996, although the April 1996 crisis alone claimed, according to Adebajo, 3,000 people in the capital.[344] The dimensions "casualties" and "number of conflict parties" are classified as "difficult" for both Abuja agreements as the number of conflict parties significantly increased due to faction splintering and new formations, which led to an intensification of fighting between 'old' and 'new' contenders of Liberian territory. The increment of factions is responsible for the "easy" value of the dimension "distribution of powers" as no faction held more than 50% of the territory. The dimension "valuable natural resources" remains

---

[340] Alao: 72, in: Accord 1996; Adebajo 2002b: 157f.
[341] Adebajo 2002b: 175.
[342] Alao: 73, in: Accord 1996; Adebajo 2002b: 184-192.
[343] Uppsala Conflict Data Program 2008: Liberia, War & Minor Conflict 1995 and 1996.
[344] Adebajo 2002b: 191f.

"difficult" from Cotonou[345] to Abuja. With three dimensions being "difficult", the nature of the conflict, hence, is classified as "difficult" for the peace agreements Abuja I and II.

The Abuja I Agreement amended and supplemented the Cotonou, Akosombo and Accra Clarification agreements. There were no changes to the disarmament and demobilization plans of the Cotonou Agreement, amended in Akosombo. The most significant contribution of the Abuja I Agreement was the agreement of the conflict parties on the composition and chairmanship of the Council of State, which had obstructed previous peace negotiations. The Council of State was extended to six members and a civilian, Wilton Sankawulo, appointed as chairman. The leader of the LPC, George Boley, was to represent the LPC/Coalition on the Council and to have equal vice-chairmanship together with Charles Taylor, Alhaji Kromah and two civilians. The idea behind the direct inclusion of the faction leaders in the Council of State was to co-opt all faction leaders with the potential to wreck the peace, excluding ULIMO-J leader Roosevelt Johnson who was granted a number of ministerial portfolios.[346] Moreover, office holders in the transitional government were permitted to contest future elections, with the condition to vacate their positions three months before the scheduled election date. A cease fire was to be in force on 26 August 1995, and the transitional government was to be installed within 14 days of the agreement with a life-span of approximately 12 months.[347] The transition government thus was to be in place twice as long as during Cotonou, providing more time for the implementation of stipulated tasks. Concerning the reform of the security sector, internal security arrangements were to be put in place, with the LNTG having the responsibility of planning the restructuring and training of the Armed Forces of Liberia.[348] Overall, the transitional government had been given a more direct role in the implementation of the agreement: for

---

[345] See also Peace Implementation Phase I for the classification of Liberia's natural resources.
[346] Alao et al. 1999: 77f.; Alao: 73, in: Accord 1996; Sesay: 23f., in: Accord 1996; Uppsala Conflict Data Program 2008: Liberia, War & Minor Conflict 1995.
[347] Alao et al. 1999: 165.
[348] ibid: 152.

example, the encampment centres were to be established by ECOMOG, UNOMIL and LNTG in collaboration with the parties.[349] The joint concept of operation, involving ECOMOG, UNOMIL and LNTG, and the clearer delineation of tasks also helped to improve coordination at different levels.[350] The previously inadequate areas spoilers and future contentious issues, however, were not amended in the first Abuja agreement.

Apart from minor amendments to the transitional government and a revised schedule of implementation, the Abuja II Agreement of 17 August 1996, most significantly, specified measures to be imposed on any faction found "guilty of acts capable of obstructing the peace plan"[351], for example, the freezing of business activities and assets in ECOWAS member states, and the exclusion from participation in the electoral process. The second Abuja agreement further earmarked several verification and assessment meetings in order to assess the progress of the different stages. Due to the improvement in the specification of the sub-goals demobilization, power sharing or political participation and reforms, the dimension "sub-goals" is classified as "medium". Under Abuja I and II, the schedule for peace implementation was more appropriate in comparison to Cotonou. The different third parties, furthermore, improved the coordination of their specific activities and worked closely together with the parties. The dimensions "schedules", "distribution of tasks", "guarantees" and "included actors" are classified as "high" for Abuja I and II. Two dimensions take different values for Abuja I and II: "future contentious issues" is valued as "low" to "medium", and "spoiler" takes "medium" to "high". As four dimensions take the value "high" and not more than one "low" with respect to Abuja I, with five dimensions taking "high" and none "low" with respect to Abuja II, the "quality of the peace agreement design" is rated as "high" for both Abuja agreements.

In February 1995, the United Nations Secretary-General Boutros Boutros-Ghali suggested the establishment of a large UN

---

[349] Alao et al. 1999: 151.
[350] ibid: 82ff.
[351] ibid: 171.

peacekeeping force under which ECOMOG was to be subsumed, which did, however, not meet approval in the Security Council. With a lack of progress in peace negotiations, in June 1995, Boutros-Ghali threatened the Liberian warring factions with a withdrawal of the remaining sixty-three UN observers. ECOWAS states warned that the withdrawal of UN observers would compromise ECOMOG efforts as the largely symbolic UN presence provided ECOMOG international legitimacy and attention.[352] In May 1995, ECOMOG's field commander General Mark Inienger called for logistical support for ECOMOG and stressed that the current 8,430 troops were not adequate for fulfilling its disarmament tasks. The high cost of maintaining ECOMOG in Liberia for five years was also imposing a high burden on contributing ECOWAS states. By August 1995, the Tanzanian and Ugandan contingents left Liberia due to financial reasons and slack of diplomatic progress, reducing ECOMOG's troop strength to 7,269.[353] The UN Secretary-General described Liberia as a "forgotten emergency" during the opening of a donor conference on assistance to Liberia on 27 October 1995. The low priority accorded to Liberia was evident in the pledge of only $145.7 million for Liberia's reconstruction although ECOWAS Chairman Jerry Rawlings had asked for $195 million for ECOMOG and UNOMIL's disarmament and demobilization tasks alone.[354] In late December 1995, ULIMO-J combatants attacked ECOMOG troops in Tubmanburg, killing sixteen peacekeepers. ECOMOG, consequently, withdrew its troops from several locations in the countryside until the safety of its troops would be guaranteed.[355] With reduced deployment to the countryside, the Abuja-mandated deadlines thus could not be met, for example, disarmament had not even begun at the time the process was to have been completed.[356]

Due to lack of commitment of the Liberian factions, the ECOWAS Heads of State of the Committee of Nine envisaged measures to be imposed on violators of the second Abuja

---

[352] Adebajo 2002b: 170f.
[353] Adebajo 2002b: 175ff.; Alao et al. 1999: 88.
[354] In comparison, the international community had pledged $6 billion for the reconstruction of Bosnia. Adebajo 2002b: 183.
[355] Adebajo 2002b: 184ff.
[356] ibid: 187f.

Agreement, including the establishment of a war crimes tribunal for Liberia.[357] The increased unity of ECOWAS member states with respect to the Liberian conflict made a credible threat of sanctions possible as the cooperation of its member states was needed for an effective imposition of sanctions. At the external level, following the April-May 1996 crisis, the United States and the European Union pledged logistical assistance to all ECOMOG contingents for the first time since its deployment.[358] The arrival of 119 trucks, helicopters and communications equipment between August and October 1996 gave ECOMOG the logistical backbone to deploy to the countryside with confidence.[359] Between February and April 1997, the arrival of Nigerian, Malian, Ghanaian, Burkinabè, Nigerien and Beninois peacekeepers and a medical team from Côte d'Ivoire increased ECOMOG's troop strength to 10,500, which enabled the peacekeeping force to maintain a presence in all thirteen counties and along the borders. The United States had been instrumental in the airlifting of the new ECOMOG contingents to Liberia, and EU member states helped cover the costs of their upkeep and provided additional funds for disarmament and the electoral process.[360] By March 1997, the United Nations also increased the number of its peacekeepers (from 23 to 93) in preparation for elections. UNOMIL, however, still had logistical and communications problems, which was related to the recovery of only 32 of its 489 vehicles looted during the crisis.[361] Shortly after the holding of elections, the mandate of UNOMIL was to be terminated: by mid-September 1997, UNOMIL had closed all its field offices and withdrawn to Monrovia for its final departure on 30 September 1997. During the ECOWAS summit meeting in August 1997, the ECOWAS Heads of State agreed to extend ECOMOG's stay in Liberia to assist in the strengthening of security and the restructuring and training of the AFL and police. The financing of these efforts was, however, not secured at the time.[362] The dimensions "provided assistance", "mandate" and

---

[357] Alao et al. 1999: 171.
[358] Adebajo 2002b: 182, 190.
[359] ibid: 207.
[360] ibid: 210f., 217f.
[361] ibid: 213.
[362] United Nations, S/RES/1116, 27 June 1997; United Nations, S/1997/712, 12 September 1997.

117

"commitment" thus take the value "medium" for both Abuja agreements. "Number of peacekeepers" and "resources" underwent an improvement from "medium" to "high": following the fighting in Monrovia, the international community began providing resources for the peace implementation tasks, and ECOMOG's troop strength reached an adequate number for the deployment throughout the country. Nonetheless, the resources were barely adequate for the transition phase, and sparsely disseminated bridging programmes did not lead to mid- to long-term reconstruction programmes. After the breakdown of Abuja I, the credible threatening of sanctions in Abuja II was to force the committal of the factions to the peace process: hence, "sanctions" are classified as "medium" to "high". As both peace implementation processes have less than four dimensions with the classification "high", the "international interest and commitment" for Abuja I and II is valued as "medium".

Action Theory

Considering the difficult nature of the conflict, high quality of the peace agreement design and medium international interest and commitment, the conditions for a successful peace implementation were better for Abuja than for Cotonou. The quality of the peace agreement design had improved with four or five respective dimensions for the Abuja agreements. Despite the higher quality of the peace agreement design, financial shortfalls hampered the implementation of Abuja I: the limited and late arrival of international assistance affected the implementation of the specified sub-goals. Despite growing war-weariness among the population as well as combatants, security could not reliably be guaranteed during the transition phase due to continued fighting in several areas in the countryside. Apart from the already hampered deployment due to lack of resources, the ongoing violence further restricted the deployment of ECOMOG and UNOMIL personnel to the countryside. A positive incentive for the option cooperation in peace implementation was that the leaders of the warring factions were directly involved in the transition government and eligible to contest for the forthcoming elections. The power-sharing guarantee had thus expanded from the inclusion of representatives of the factions in the transitional government to the direct seating of warring faction leaders in the Council of State. Due to the inadequate international commitment and interest and the corresponding inadequate provision of security during peace implementation, the benefit of continued war activities was higher than the benefit of the option peace implementation for Abuja I. The lack of adequately provided security became glaring during the outbreak of intensified fighting in the capital, which led to a high number of casualties and the looting and destruction of property in the presence of sub-regional peacekeepers.

The increased international assistance received for the implementation of Abuja II, the threatening of sanctions to violators of the peace agreement provisions and the deployment of peacekeepers to all Liberian counties were more favourable conditions for peace implementation. The deployment of peacekeepers throughout Liberia and along the borders with its neighbouring countries restricted commercial activities as well as new territorial conquests of the different warring factions. The status quo could thus not be improved through the continuance of war activities. The resumption of war activities would, on the contrary, have had negative implications for the warring faction engaged in this spoiling behaviour as the costs would have included, for example, the exclusion from the electoral process, and the restriction of its economic activities through the freezing of its assets. The worst consequence would have been the trial in front of a war crimes tribunal for Liberia. With the resigning of their positions in the transitional government for participation in the forthcoming elections, the leaders of the warring factions demonstrated that their interest in political contest was higher than continued contest on the battlefield. With respect to Abuja II, the warring factions thus preferred the course of action H1 Cooperation in peace implementation to H2 Non-cooperation in peace implementation.

Dependent Variable

The implementation of Abuja I proved difficult in the face of the low international assistance provided to ECOMOG. The delayed deployment of ECOMOG troops made the initiating of tasks such as disarmament impossible. Despite the proper delineation of procedures and tasks, the means, moreover, were not available for their implementation. For example, there were no resources to maintain encampment sites for the proposed period of two to four months or even for a shorter time. A much greater stumbling block was the sharp increase of cease-fire violations following the signing of the agreement, and, due to continued distrust and confrontation, the warring factions did not disengage. The phases following disengagement, such as assembly, encampment, disarmament and demobilization, thus could not begin.[363] Political differences, moreover, hampered the smooth functioning of the transitional government, especially regarding the allocation of posts. The faction leaders also attempted to increase their authority by determining the council to be a collective presidency, responsible for disarming fighters as well as approving ECOMOG's deployment plans. Hence, with all dimensions, except "power sharing/political participation", taking the value "low", Abuja I failed in the implementation of the most important sub-goals: disarmament and demobilization were not started, which was largely due to the failure of the warring factions to disengage and the financial and logistical shortcomings of ECOMOG and UNOMIL. The other processes dependent on the success of disarmament and demobilization could thus not be implemented. The constant cease-fire violations following the signing of the first Abuja agreement culminated in large-scale violence in Monrovia in April-May 1996, with 3000 casualties estimated for this period alone, marking the death of Abuja I. Victor Gbeho described the ensuing cease fire as a product of factional fatigue and diminution in resources than the result of mediation attempts by ECOWAS, which could not bring the warlords back to the negotiating table until late July 1996.[364]

---

[363] Alao et al. 1999: 84-88; Adebajo 2002b: 188.
[364] Adebajo 2002b: 191-195.

Attempts to restore the momentum of the peace process resulted in the signing of Abuja II, which revised the implementation schedule of the first Abuja agreement. The progress of each of its five stages was to be monitored and assessed by ECOWAS, which was authorized to recommend sanctions against violators of the cease fire.[365] The prospects for peace implementation were, however, adverse because the materials and goods intended for disarmament and demobilization were completely looted during the April crisis.[366] Given the lack of resources and inadequate troop strength of both ECOMOG and UNOMIL, encampment could not be conducted. The overall time spent by a fighter at disarmament and demobilization sites was also significantly reduced in comparison to original plans. The arrival of logistical support between August and October 1996 enabled ECOMOG's deployment to disarmament sites throughout the country. The disarmament process started on schedule and resulted, according to UN figures, to the disarming and demobilizing of 24,500 of estimated 33,000 combatants. In exchange for handing in a serviceable weapon or a hundred rounds of ammunition to ECOMOG, the fighters received food rations and were transported to a community of their choice. In comparison to the disarming of 11,553 of 12,500 NPFL fighters, the smaller factions ULIMO-J and LPC were more reluctant, fearing a higher loss if fighting was to resume. Demobilization was also more successful in areas controlled either by ECOMOG or by a single warring faction than in resources-rich areas that continued to be militarily contested. ECOMOG's establishment of buffer zones between the two ULIMO factions in the northwest and between the NPFL and LPC in the southeast by the end of disarmament on 31 January 1997 contributed to the fact that no cease-fire violations were reported between 12 January and 19 March 1997.[367] There was, however, not much emphasis placed on reintegration during peace implementation of Abuja II: in January 1997, the only available reintegration programme was a three-

---

[365] Alao et al. 1999: 90; Adebajo 2002b: 194ff., 208f.
[366] Alao et al. 1999: 90-93.
[367] Alao et al. 1999: 94ff.; Adebajo 2002a: 63f.

month bridging programme, involving road clearing and bridge mending, which was just coming off on a small scale.[368]

Figure 4.13   Disarmament process[369]

The new chair of the Council of State, Ruth Perry, proved to be more energetic than Wilton Sankawulo in rallying support for the Liberian peace process domestically and abroad. However, the three warlords continued to block serious dialogue on key issues

[368] Alao et al. 1999: 94ff.
[369] CNN 1997c.

of the peace process. An assassination attempt on Charles Taylor in October 1996 led to the suspension of the council until a reconciliation of the warlords in January 1997 made a reconvening of the council possible.[370]

Figure 4.14   Election campaign, 1997[371]

As early as 22 February 1996, the Liberian opposition decided to unite in order to defeat Charles Taylor's National Patriotic Party (NPP) at the polls. However, by the time of the election, the seven-party-alliance had reduced to an alliance of two, largely due to disagreement on the choice of Cletus Wotorson as presidential candidate.[372] Ellen Johnson-Sirleaf joined the presidential race on 18 April 1997. She had opposed ECOMOG's intervention in 1990 and initially supported the NPFL in its attempt to overthrow Doe. She was considered the favoured candidate of the United States, while Nigeria was seen to prefer Taylor for the reason that his victory seemed the only way Liberia would return to a state of peace.[373] The ECOWAS summit of 21 May 1997 postponed the elections from May to July 1997 to provide more time for electoral preparations. Owing to the high number of internally displaced Liberians, a system of proportional representation was decided to be the most appropriate. About 75,000 of over 550,000 refugees in neighbouring states returned home to participate in the

---

[370] Adebajo 2002b: 208.
[371] CNN 1997a, b.
[372] Adebajo 2002b: 208.
[373] Adebajo 2002b: 218-222; Alao et al. 1999: 102-107.

elections.[374] On 19 July 1997, Liberian voters cast ballots with ECOMOG providing security at the 1,864 voting stations and more than 500 international and 1,300 local observers monitoring the election. Charles Taylor won a landslide victory of 75.3 percent, while Ellen Johnson-Sirleaf won 9.5 percent of the presidential vote. ECOWAS and the United Nations issued a joint statement, declaring the election "free and fair". Taylor's election was attributed to the fact that many Liberians saw him as a guarantor of peace, fearing a return to war if he lost. With Taylor's margin of victory, his party took nearly total control of the bicameral legislature, winning 21 out of 26 Senate seats and 49 of 64 seats in the House of Representatives. There was a consequential fear that "a strong government might ultimately strangle any meaningful opposition"[375]. With renewed confidence after successful elections, ECOMOG committed itself to remaining in Liberia for additional six months to assist in the rebuilding of a new army and the provision of security.[376] The implementation of Abuja II can be classified as "success" as the four sub-goals of top priority were implemented during the transition phase, leading to Liberia's first elections after 1985. The lack of implementation of the other sub-goals, however, hindered the country from moving from peace implementation to peace consolidation. A longer commitment of third parties to Liberia might have abetted the institution of reforms, regulation of the trade in natural resources and rehabilitation of ex-combatants and displaced civilians through substantial programmes.

Summary

The Abuja I Agreement solved and at the same time created new problems: the appointed neutral chair of the Council of State, which was to mediate between the warlords, could not exert any influence on the warlords. Whilst the leaders of the warring factions thrived for a political solution as members of the Council

---

[374] Adebajo 2002a: 65f., 211ff.
[375] Alao et al. 1999: 107.
[376] Alao et al. 1999: 102-109; Adebajo 2002a: 65f., 211ff.; Adebajo 2002b: 218-222.

of State, they continued to pursue their territorial and commercial interests.[377] The warlords' presence in the capital also led to an increase in combatants in Monrovia, which had security implications for the further development of the implementation phase. Additionally, the pledged international assistance did not arrive at the beginning of the implementation phase and hindered the start of demobilization, disarmament and encampment. Six months after the signing of the agreement, the peace process came to a standstill. Severe violations of the cease fire culminated in the outbreak of fractional fighting in the capital. In comparison, the Abuja agreement of August 1996 resulted in the highest degree of demobilisation and disarmament so far and paved the way for the elections in July 1997. Changes were, among others, the consideration of sanctions for violations of the agreement provisions and the appointment of a new chair for the Council of State. The beforehand pledged international assistance for Abuja I, furthermore, began arriving during the Abuja II implementation. Despite this support, ECOMOG and UNOMIL still remained understaffed and underfinanced, which led to modifications of the peace plan: the planned encampment was cancelled, and the focus was laid on the disarmament and demobilization of combatants. The elections had to be postponed due to the adjustment of the implementation schedule and the reform of the electoral system. The elections were successfully conducted but there were fears that Taylor's landslide victory would have consequences for the control function of the opposition and that security institutions would solely reflect the interests of the NPP.[378]

Peace Implementation Phase III: Accra Agreement (2003)

Following the elections of 1997, the former warlord established an authoritarian-repressive presidential regime[379]: President Taylor soon cracked down on any critics, seeking to

---

[377] Kamara 2002: 23.
[378] Adebajo 2002a: 59-73; cf. Alao 1999 et al.
[379] Hofmeier/Mehler 2004: 173.

institutionalize his dominance of the Liberian state. On 12 November 1998, Taylor accused 32 people, including former warlords, of participating in a conspiracy to toppling his government.[380] Furthermore, the former warlord strengthened his executive power by transferring the sole power of allotting concessions for the extraction of Liberia's "strategic commodities" to the president.[381] With a lack of progress regarding security and human rights, pledged financial support by international donors for Liberia's reconstruction was never made available to Taylor's regime.[382] Following the election, Taylor refused ECOMOG's assistance in the restructuring and training of Liberia's security forces and replaced demobilized officers with former NPFL fighters. By the end of 1998, ECOMOG had withdrawn all their peacekeepers from Liberia as Taylor's continuing support of RUF rebels in Sierra Leone had soured relations between Taylor and ECOMOG.[383] In April 1999, Liberian dissidents, Liberians United for Reconciliation and Democracy (LURD), crossed the Northern border of Liberia from Guinea, launching attacks on Taylor's forces. The conflict escalated along the border between Liberia and Guinea in September 1999. Meanwhile, there was increasing external pressure on Taylor to stop the military assistance to RUF rebels in Sierra Leone, with the United Nations Security Council imposing its first secondary sanctions against a country supporting rebels in a neighbouring state.[384] With LURD and Movement of Democracy in Liberia (MODEL) rebels reaching Monrovia in mid-2003, Taylor's government was forced to enter into peace negotiations with the rebel groups. On 17 June 2003, the government and rebel groups signed a cease fire agreement, which called for the establishment of an interim government within 30 days, excluding Charles Taylor. On 11 August 2003, Taylor stepped down as president of Liberia and left the country for exile in Nigeria.[385] One significant change to the first civil war was the higher involvement of the United Nations in the

---

[380] Levitt 2005: 211-214.
[381] Global Witness 2001d: 8.
[382] Adebajo 2002a: 67-73.
[383] ibid: 68f.
[384] Levitt 2005: 215f.; United Nations, S/RES/1343, 7 March 2001.
[385] Levitt 2005: 237; Adebajo: 294, in: Adebajo/Rashid 2004.

settlement of the conflict, with the establishment of the United Nations Mission in Liberia (UNMIL).[386] The Accra Agreement further sought to advance a higher inclusion of political parties and civil society groups in the transitional government. Nonetheless, differences between representatives of LURD and MODEL with Chairman Gyude Bryant over ministerial positions, and themes of governance and impunity affected the workings of the transitional government. With the full deployment of UNMIL and international management of Liberia's resources, the implementation of planned programmes and reforms was rendered possible, paving the way for the general elections of October 2005.[387]

Independent Variables

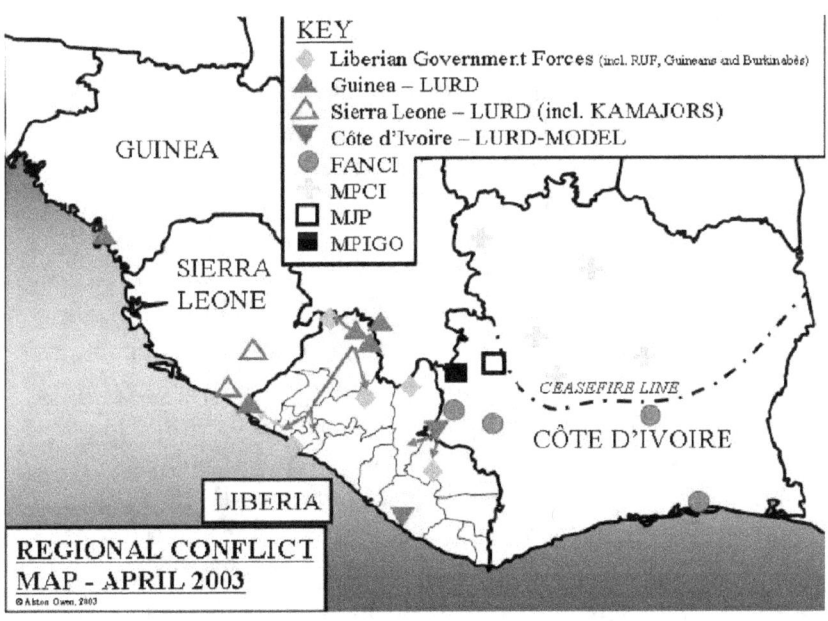

Map 4.9   Regional Conflict, April 2003[388]

---

[386] United Nations, S/RES/1509, 19 September 2003.
[387] United Nations, S/2005/391, 16 June 2005; International Crisis Group 2005: 1f.
[388] International Crisis Group 2003a: 37.

The continuing instability at the Guinea-Liberia border led the governments in Guinea and Liberia to support rival rebel movements against each other's regimes. In retaliation for Taylor's backing of Guinean rebel groups, in 2001, the Guinea government allegedly began supplying LURD with arms and ammunition in exchange for coffee, cocoa and diamonds.[389] The LURD was essentially "a loose coalition of anti-Taylor forces, drawing upon a variety of militia factions and refugee groups, increasingly backed by Guinea, with more indirect support from Sierra Leone, the U.S. and Great Britain"[390]. President Taylor appealed to the UN Security Council for the lifting of sanctions imposed against Liberia on 7 May 2001 in view of Guinea and Sierra Leone supporting LURD. His request was, however, turned down based on his continued support for the RUF against the elected Sierra Leonean government.[391] Charles Taylor supported rebels in western Côte d'Ivoire, partly from desire to remove Ivorian president Laurent Gbagbo but also to protect a major arms supply and timber trade route to the Ivorian port San Pedro. By May 2001, the LURD had firm control of Lofa County and reached 50 miles to the capital in January 2002. In response, President Taylor urged former NPFL allies to take up arms against LURD. By September 2002, the Liberian government had gained some ground. A group closely associated with LURD, MODEL, was armed by President Gbagbo, fighting alongside Ivorian government loyalist forces in Côte d'Ivoire and launching attacks into eastern Liberia in January and February 2003 (Map 4.9).[392] By the start of April 2003, LURD controlled three major axes leading toward Monrovia, while MODEL attacks had weakened government positions in the southeast. By late April, the situation in Liberia had caught attention of the international community as the humanitarian crisis reached catastrophic levels, with humanitarian agencies unable to access 70 percent of the country. 60 percent of Liberia was then under rebel control.[393] The Uppsala Conflict Data Program estimates between 1661 and

---

[389] Adebajo: 294, 298, in: Adebajo/Rashid 2004; Levitt 2005: 215-219; Adebajo 2002a: 68f.
[390] International Crisis Group 2002a: 4.
[391] Adebajo: 294, 298, in: Adebajo/Rashid 2004; Levitt 2005: 215-219; United Nations, S/RES/1343, 7 March 2001; Adebajo 2002a: 68f.
[392] International Crisis Group 2003a: 1ff., 19.
[393] Levitt 2005: 223; United Nations, S/2003/466, 22 April 2003.

2278 battle-related deaths for the year 2003, thus classifying this period as "war". The advancing of LURD fighters into western suburbs of Monrovia by June 2003 resulted in heavy fighting around the capital and several casualties, with more than 2000 battle-related deaths counted for fighting between LURD and government forces in Monrovia alone.[394] The figures are, however, still thought to be on the lower side: both sides committed numerous human rights abuses, including summary killings, which might not all be reflected in the counted numbers.[395] Hence, all dimensions of the variable "nature of the conflict" take the value "difficult": more than two conflict parties were contending for power, which enjoyed the support of various neighbouring states and the lootability of present valuable natural resources[396] for their ends. By April 2003, more than 50% of the Liberian territory was in the hands of rebels, with the contest for Monrovia increasing the number of overall casualties by thousands. With more than three dimensions classified as "difficult", the "nature of the conflict" is "difficult" for the Accra peace agreement.

The Ceasefire Agreement of 17 June 2003 called for an immediate ceasefire, secured by an interim interposition force established by ECOWAS. A Joint Monitoring Committee (JMC) was to supervise the implementation of the Ceasefire Agreement and resolve disputes concerning any alleged cease-fire violations.[397] The parties to the Accra peace agreement, signed on 18 August 2003, called for the establishment of an International Stabilization Force (ISF), which was, among others, to conduct the disarmament of combatants. Following disengagement, the forces were to move to cantonment sites before proceeding on to reintegration activities. A National Commission for Disarmament, Demobilization, Rehabilitation and Reintegration (NCDDRR) was to coordinate these processes. The Agreement further stipulated the reforming and restructuring of the national army and police force and established a Governance Reform

---

[394] Uppsala Conflict Data Program 2008: Liberia, War & Minor Conflict 2003.
[395] Levitt 2005: 219-225; International Crisis Group 2003a: 8.
[396] See also Peace Implementation Phase I for the classification of Liberia's natural resources.
[397] United Nations, S/2003/850, 29 August 2003, pp. 28-34.

Commission and Contract and Monopolies Commission for the improvement of the governance sector.[398] The two-year transition period was to be governed by a power-sharing government, the National Transitional Government of Liberia (NTGL). In comparison to earlier peace agreements, a greater focus was laid on civil society representation in the transitional government, reserving the transitional chairmanship and vice-chairmanship to representatives of civil society. The legislative branch of the NTGL was to reflect a broad spectrum of the Liberian society, with the assignment of seats to the Government of Liberia (GOL), LURD, MODEL, political parties, civil society and special interest groups, and Liberia's 15 counties. As an improvement to preceding peace agreements, the allocation of ministerial and other positions, and a detailed implementation timetable for the agreement were already at hand at the signing of the agreement. The presidential and general elections scheduled for October 2003 were postponed to a date not later than October 2005, providing ample time for the reform of the electoral system.[399] Concerning post-conflict rehabilitation and reconstruction, the signatories called for the establishment of a United Nations Mission in Liberia with the adequate resources to "facilitate the implementation and coordination of the Political, Social, Economic and Security assistance to be extended under this Agreement"[400]. An Implementation Monitoring Committee (IMC) was to ensure the "effective and faithful" implementation of the peace agreement. Any dispute with regard to the application or interpretation of the agreement provisions were to be settled through mediation efforts by ECOWAS. The Agreement further included agreements on the repatriation of refugees and IDP's, the establishing of a human rights commission and truth and reconciliation commission. With the specification of demobilization, disarmament, power sharing or political participation, elections and reforms in the Accra Agreement, the dimension "sub-goals" takes the value "high".

---

[398] United Nations, S/2003/850, 29 August 2003, pp. 4-10; Uppsala Conflict Data Program 2008: Liberia, Peace Agreement 2003.
[399] United Nations, S/2003/850, 29 August 2003, pp. 13-20; Uppsala Conflict Data Program 2008: Liberia, Peace Agreement 2003.
[400] United Nations, S/2003/850, 29 August 2003, p. 21.

The sub-goal reintegration was partly specified through the establishment of the NCDDRR and the formation of a new army, which was to incorporate qualified ex-combatants as well as civilians. The two-year transition period provided adequate time for the implementation of the agreement provisions, including the initiating of specified reforms. The tasks of the different implementing bodies – ECOWAS, NTGL and the requested International Stabilization Force under the auspices of a comprehensive United Nations Mission in Liberia – were also adequately specified. The power-sharing government further guaranteed the inclusion of all relevant Liberian parties at this stage of the peace process. Despite the establishment of mechanisms and commissions with regard to future contentious issues, consequences for violators of agreed provisions were neither stipulated in the ceasefire nor the peace agreement. With only the dimension "spoiler" taking the value "low", the quality of the Accra Agreement is classified as "high".

Figure 4.15 Delayed U.S. involvement[401]

Owing to Taylor's responsibility for regional destabilization and earlier business connections with al-Qaeda, the U.S. government, according to the International Crisis Group, played a central part

---

[401] BBC 2003c.

in his overthrow. A military source went as far as describing LURD as "a creation of the American secret services"[402]. At any rate, the U.S. authorities were aware of Guinea's arming of LURD and the simultaneous build-up of MODEL by Côte d'Ivoire as well as the planned LURD offensive on Monrovia. On the date of the LURD offensive, the Sierra Leone Special Court indicted Charles Taylor for war crimes and requested Switzerland to freeze all accounts held by Charles Taylor, his relatives and members of his government due to proceeds received from Sierra Leonean diamonds in exchange for support to the RUF.[403] The Taylor government, moreover, battled with the effects of sanctions imposed on Liberia due to its continuous support for armed factions in the sub-region. Sanctions imposed under Security Council Resolution 1343 (6 May 2001) included travel restrictions on senior members of Taylor's government, a ban on direct and indirect import of rough diamonds, an arms embargo and the grounding of all Liberian aircraft. A ban on round logs and timber products was added in May 2003 (Security Council Resolution 1478), with a demand on the Liberian government to demonstrate that revenues derived from the timber industry and the Liberia Ship and Corporate Registry were used for legitimate social, humanitarian and development purposes.[404] Due to the worsened humanitarian situation in Liberia in mid-2003, UN Secretary-General Kofi Annan called for a multinational intervention force in Liberia, suggesting that this force be led by a permanent member. President George W. Bush urged Charles Taylor to resign but refrained from committing the U.S. to a further role in the conflict.[405] Security Council Resolution 1497 (2003) authorized the establishment of a multinational force with the task of supporting the implementation of the Ceasefire Agreement, with UNAMSIL to provide logistical support to forward ECOWAS elements.[406] On 4 August 2003, the first group of Economic Community of West African States (ECOWAS) Mission in Liberia (ECOMIL) peacekeepers arrived

---

[402] International Crisis Group 2003b: 14f.
[403] International Crisis Group 2003b: 14f.; Levitt 2005: 227.
[404] International Crisis Group 2003b: 15f.; United Nations, S/RES/1343, 7 March 2001; United Nations, S/RES/1478, 6 May 2003.
[405] Levitt 2005: 227ff.
[406] United Nations, S/RES/1497, 1 August 2003.

in Liberia (Figure 4.16). By mid-September 2003, ECOMIL had about 3,500 peacekeepers on the ground, comprising contingents from Benin, Gambia, Ghana, Guinea-Bissau, Mali, Nigeria, Senegal and Togo.

Figure 4.16   Welcoming of ECOMIL peacekeepers, August 2003[407]

---

[407] BBC 2003c.

The United States provided logistical support to ECOMIL troops and sent a naval ship off the coast of Liberia, with about 200 U.S. Marines helping ECOMIL in distributing humanitarian aid.[408] On 19 September 2003, the UN Security Council unanimously approved the formation of a 15,000-strong peacekeeping force for Liberia with Chapter VII enforcement powers, along with a 1,115-strong civilian police component. The United Nations Mission in Liberia (UNMIL) was established for a period of 12 months and given the mandate to support the implementation of the Ceasefire Agreement and the overall peace process, including assisting the transitional government in asserting their nationwide authority and in the restructuring of Liberia's police force and military; and support humanitarian and human rights assistance. The mandate further required UNMIL to aid the transitional government in restoring proper administration of Liberia's natural resources. UNMIL began its mission on 1 October 2003, with ECOMIL forces being incorporated into UNMIL.[409]

Despite the withdrawal of U.S. troops after UNMIL's takeover, the United States pledged to support UNMIL financially, provide officers to UNMIL headquarters and help restructure and train a new Liberian army.[410] Turning the comprehensive UNMIL mandate into reality proved difficult at the initial stage as the process of generating peacekeeping troops was moving slower than anticipated. As at 12 December 2003 (Map 4.10), the troop strength of UNMIL only stood at 5,900 military personnel. The thin troop strength hampered UNMIL's efforts to deploy beyond Monrovia and delayed disarmament and demobilization programmes.[411] Owing to inadequate numbers of peacekeepers and lack of adequate planning, the disarmament process collapsed in December 2003 amid clashes between forces loyal to the former government of Liberia and UNMIL's peacekeepers.

---

[408] Levitt 2005: 238, 240f.; International Crisis Group 2003b: 13; United Nations, S/2003/1175, 15 December 2003.
[409] United Nations, S/RES/1509, 19 September 2003; Levitt 2005: 240f.; International Crisis Group 2003b: 15.
[410] International Crisis Group 2003b: 2, 15.
[411] United Nations, S/2003/1175, 15 December 2003, I, II.

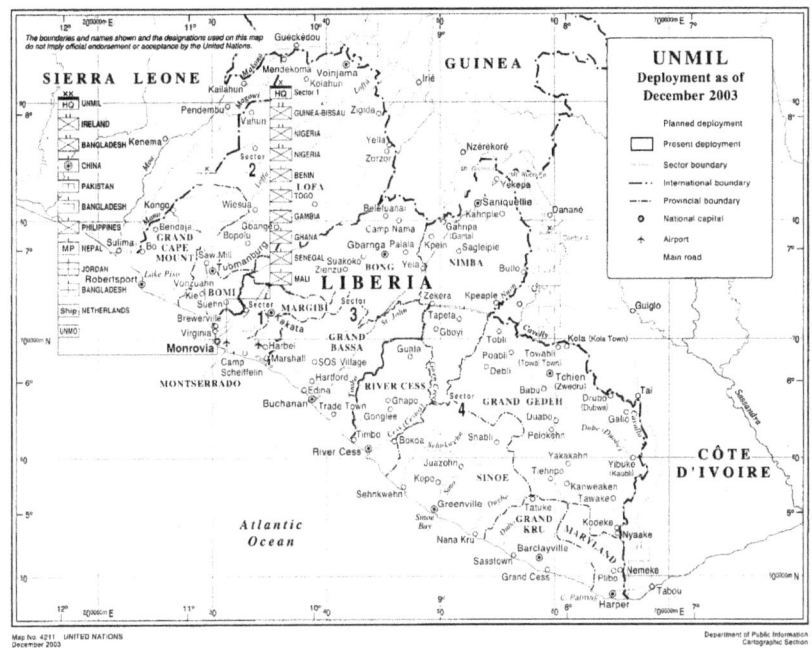

Map 4.10   UNMIL deployment, December 2003[412]

As a consequence, the pace of troop deployment gathered momentum with the arrival of contingents from Bangladesh, Ethiopia, Ireland, Namibia and Pakistan, bringing UNMIL's troop strength to 12,731 by March 2004.[413] The arrival of further contingents in late March and April 2004 enabled UNMIL to deploy throughout Liberia and re-launch the disarmament, demobilization, rehabilitation and reintegration (DDRR) programme.[414] UNMIL reached its near-total authorized troop strength by August 2004 (Map 4.11).[415] Whilst pledges towards Liberia's short- to medium-term reconstruction and development needs totalled $522, the consolidated appeal for humanitarian activities in Liberia remained underfunded. Financial shortfalls further delayed the provision of reintegration possibilities, restructuring of the military and improvement of conditions in

[412] United Nations, S/2003/1175, 15 December 2003.
[413] International Crisis Group 2004a: 1; United Nations, S/2004/229, 22 March 2004, II.
[414] United Nations, S/2004/430, 26 May 2004, II, V.
[415] United Nations, S/2004/725, 10 September 2004, II.

Liberia's correctional facilities.[416] The dimensions "provided assistance" and "resources" can be classified "medium" to "high": although appropriate resources and pledged assistance arrived later than anticipated, the timely arrival of ECOMIL forces stabilized the volatile situation following the signing of the Ceasefire Agreement. UNMIL comprised the largest UN peacekeeping mission up till then with a comprehensive, tough mandate. Its comprehensive mandate and the sanctions imposed on Liberia formed the backbone for the Mission's leverage during the peace implementation phase. UNMIL's wide-ranging tasks underlined not only a comprehensive mandate but also a longer commitment to Liberia. With more than four dimensions falling into the category "high", the international interest and commitment is, consequently, "high" for the peace implementation phase III.

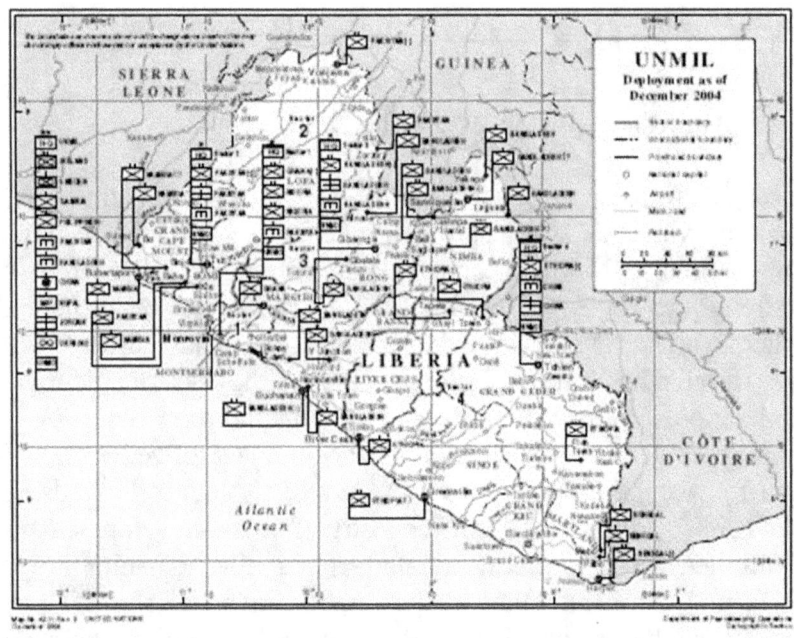

Map 4.11   UNMIL deployment, December 2004[417]

---

[416] United Nations, S/2004/229, 22 March 2004, XIII, XVI; United Nations, S/2004/725, 10 September 2004, V, XVII.
[417] United Nations, S/2004/972, 17 December 2004.

Action Theory

The increased international interest and commitment towards settling the second Liberian civil war was a favourable condition for negotiating and implementing the Accra Agreement. The significant loss of territory to the rebel groups LURD and MODEL, and the increased international pressure on Charles Taylor made the Government of Liberia and President Charles Taylor more accessible to negotiations. The rebel groups, on the other hand, went confidently into the peace negotiations, expecting to reap all the benefits in return for their input in overthrowing Taylor. The peace agreement, however, restricted the role of the warring factions in the transitional government in stipulating that the chairman and vice-chairman positions were to be given to a civilian, and the ministerial positions were divided among the warring factions, the government of Liberia, political parties and civil society. This restriction was only made possible through the strong, long-term commitment of the international community to Liberia's reconstruction. The high international commitment also expressed itself in the quality of the peace agreement design as only the deployment of a peacekeeping mission with adequate resources and personnel was to make the implementation of the comprehensive peace agreement possible. The delayed arrival of international assistance and peacekeepers, however, hampered the initial implementation of the specified sub-goals. Security could thus not be guaranteed beyond Monrovia and its surroundings until the arrival of further contingents in early 2004 significantly increased UNMIL's troop strength, which enabled the Mission to deploy to the interior, guarantee security throughout Liberia and re-launch the disarmament programme. The increased monitoring of Liberia's border areas by UNMIL, in collaboration with UN missions in Sierra Leone and Côte d'Ivoire, also restricted the moving of combatants and weapons within the sub-region, thus cutting off further war-related activities of Liberian combatants in neighbouring states. The resumption of war activities and spoiling behaviour would, moreover, have had negative consequences for the warring factions due to the increased international monitoring of the peace process and tough stance towards spoilers in the transitional government, leading to their suspension. With UNMIL attaining its total authorized troop strength thus came a higher collaboration of the warring factions towards the implementation of the Agreement's sub-goals. Alternatives to warfare were, furthermore, provided to ex-combatants in the form of bridging programmes and education opportunities for child soldiers, whilst reintegration programmes were to be introduced with the arrival of adequate funds. Owing to the strong international commitment and high quality of the peace agreement, marked by negative consequences for spoilers and positive incentives for collaborators, the benefit of the course of action H1 Cooperation in peace implementation was thus higher for the warring factions than H2 Non-cooperation in peace implementation.

Dependent Variable

Owing to the slow arrival of peacekeepers to Liberia, the implementation of the Accra Agreement initially got into great difficulties. UNMIL remained in Monrovia and its surroundings in 2003, awaiting the arrival of further contingents before the extension of its deployment. UNMIL took a risk in starting disarmament in December 2003 without enough peacekeepers and adequate mechanisms in place. UNMIL peacekeepers were not ready at the starting day of the disarmament programme (7 December 2003), resulting in the breakout of riots and demonstrations against UNMIL troops at Camp Scheiffelin where many Government of Liberia (GOL) fighters had assembled for disarmament. As a result, disarmament and demobilization were suspended on 17 December 2003.[418] With the arrival of additional contingents, UNMIL deployed to some key areas by mid-January 2004, including the LURD strongholds Tubmanburg and Gbarnga, and Buchanan and Zwedru held by MODEL.[419] Significant progress in UNMIL attaining its authorized troop strength, coupled with its deployment throughout Liberia and increment of air and road patrols, contributed to improved security and enabled the re-launching of the disarmament,

---

[418] United Nations, S/2003/1175, 15 December 2003; International Crisis Group 2004a: 1, 4ff.
[419] International Crisis Group 2004a: 1f.

demobilization, reintegration and rehabilitation (DDRR) programme on 18 April 2004. UNMIL initially estimated the number of combatants at about 17,000 and doubled the number in order to accommodate more war-affected people, especially women and children. Almost 104,000 entered the programme, including an assumed high number of foreign combatants and non-combatants. Originally anticipated as a three-week process, demobilization was reduced to three days completing questionnaires and waiting for the initial U.S. $150 payment at cantonment sites. The DD programme officially ended on 31 October 2004, resulting in the disarmament and demobilization of 101,449 combatants, and the collection of 33,000 heavy munitions and 7 million rounds of small ammunition.[420] The payment of U.S. $300 demobilization packages to the inflated number of combatants contributed to the shortage of funds for the subsequent reintegration programme. Owing to inadequate funding, the implementation of the reintegration programme proceeded at a very slow pace, with 70,000 combatants still seeking to benefit from it in late 2004. By the end of 2005, the number dropped to 26,000. The completion of the programme was in particular vital in order to combat the problems of re-recruitment of fighters, illegal exploitation of natural resources and increment of violent crime.[421]

On 14 October 2003, Gyude Bryant, a neutral businessman, was sworn in as the head of the transitional government. His first actions included abolishing monopolies on imports of rice and petroleum products that had been put in place by Charles Taylor. Owing to manipulations of the warring factions, the civilian chairman had, however, difficulties in pushing through institutional reforms and exercising the authority accorded to him by the peace agreement. A major issue was the battle over positions in the transitional government, with the warring factions claiming that they were accorded the right to decide on all deputy and assistant ministers in Accra. On 7 January 2004, Bryant awarded 51 out of 86 assistant minister positions "for the sake of peace" as it had stalled any productive

---

[420] United Nations, S/2004/972, 17 December 2004; International Crisis Group 2009: 27f.
[421] International Crisis Group 2009: 28; United Nations, S/2004/725, 10 September 2004; United Nations, S/2005/560, 1 September 2005.

decision-making in the transitional government.[422] According to Jacques Paul Klein, the Special Representative of the UN Secretary General (SRSG) to Liberia, as of 15 September 2004, some factions and members of the NTGL still lacked political commitment, and corruption and lack of transparency by the transitional government in the management of public funds remained serious concerns.[423]

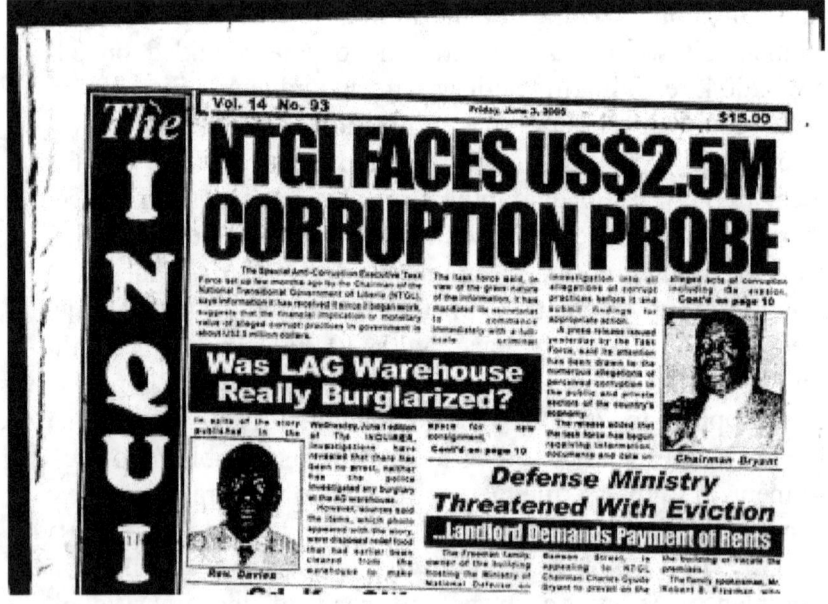

Figure 4.17   Corruption charges[424]

By February 2005, the dynamic shifted with the press and civil society organisations accusing NTGL members of financial malfeasance – from theft of millions of dollars to the issuance of illegal contracts, leading to the suspension and trial of several officials (Figure 4.17). On the basis of investigations carried out by ECOWAS and the European Commission, donors and diplomatic communities demanded intrusive measures to strengthen economic governance and prevent corruption. The Liberian Governance and Economic Management Assistance

---

[422] International Crisis Group 2004a: 1f., 8f., 13f.
[423] International Crisis Group 2004b: 1, 27.
[424] Global Witness 2005d: 39.

Plan (GEMAP) was, subsequently, signed in September 2005 by the NTGL and the International Contact Group of Liberia.[425] The NTGL also showed a lack of political willingness to implement measures for the adequate control and management of natural resources. Out of this reason, the Security Council extended timber and diamond sanctions levied on Liberia during Taylor's regime until necessary measures for the responsible administration of these state revenues were in place.[426] Owing to failed progress during the transition phase, they were only lifted during the term of the first elected government. The timber sanctions were nullified by Security Council Resolution 1689 (2006) due to the incumbent government's commitment to transparent management of its forestry resources and its progress in instituting reforms in the timber sector. Security Council Resolution 1752 (2007) terminated the diamond sanctions on Liberia, owing to progress in putting in place the requirements of the Kimberley Process Certification Scheme.[427]

Between November 2003 and June 2004, an interim police force of 646 officers was trained by the United Nations to perform policing functions in Monrovia pending the formation of a new, restructured police force. The NTGL and UNMIL launched the recruitment process for the new force on 5 May 2004, with training commencing for a first group of 132 cadets in July 2004. The three-month programme involved academic training, followed by a six-month on-the-job training.[428] The target of 1,800 trained Liberian National Police (LNP) personnel was achieved by the time of the October elections. 300 police personnel received crowd control training in Nigeria, which were to form a police support unit handling riot control and violent crime. The vetting and training process for personnel from other law enforcement agencies also commenced during the transition phase. Despite this significant progress, further funding was required for bringing the number of trained LNP personnel to the provisional full strength of 3,500, the rehabilitation of police

---

[425] International Crisis Group 2005: 1f., 10ff.; United Nations, S/2005/560, 1 September 2005, II.
[426] United Nations, S/RES/1521, 22 December 2003; United Nations, S/2005/391, 16 June 2005.
[427] United Nations, S/2005/560, 1 September 2005, XIII; United Nations, S/RES/1689, 20 June 2006; United Nations, S/RES/1753, 27 April 2007.
[428] United Nations, S/2004/430, 26 May 2004; United Nations, S/2004/725, 10 September 2004; United Nations, S/2004/972, 17 December 2004.

infrastructure and the demobilization of redundant or ineligible personnel.[429]

Figure 4.18   Recruitment of new army personnel[430]

The programme to restructure the Armed Forces of Liberia (AFL), led by the United States, made less progress during the transition phase. Delays were attributed to funding shortfalls, the nature of the U.S. State Department's contracting system and the complex dynamics between Liberian and international actors, especially with regard to the training curriculum. DynCorp, a private company, was given the contract to reform the Liberian military. Before the commencing of training, DynCorp had to demobilize the former AFL and the defence ministry (MoD), with the arrangement of demobilization payments taking up most of 2006 as well as the refurbishing of training facilities. The basic training eventually commenced in August 2006, consisting of eight weeks of marksmanship with AK-47s, use of hand grenades, physical, hygiene and first aid training, map reading and drills. The new AFL was to reach an overall troop strength of

---

[429] United Nations, S/2005/764, 7 December 2005.
[430] Global Witness 2006e: 8.

2,000, with the U.S.-funded training to finish by early 2010.[431] The justice sector remained ineffective, owing to a lack of funding, institutional capacity, facilities, as well as qualified prosecutors and defence counsel. UNMIL assisted in reopening the Arthur Grimes School of Law, trained public prosecutors and corrections officers, and oversaw quick impact projects for the refurbishment of court structures in Liberia's thirteen counties and improved conditions in correctional facilities. Serious concerns, however, remained in particular with regard to dismal conditions in corrections establishments and long periods of prisoners in pre-trial detention due to the overwhelmed justice system.[432]

The electoral process started on 25 April 2005 with voter registration. According to the constitution, the delineation of electoral districts was to be based on a census, which had to be ruled out due to time constraints, relying instead on the number of registered voters in the respective districts. The quality of the registration process was generally assessed as good, except with regard to internally displaced people as the return to their communities and voter registration occurred simultaneously. The preparations for the elections, on the whole, were competent and transparent, with the National Electoral Commission (NEC) maintaining a high level of neutrality. Twenty-two (22) presidential and 22 vice-presidential candidates, 206 senatorial candidates and 512 candidates for the House of Representatives were approved by the NEC. The electoral campaign began on 15 August 2005 (Figure 4.19).[433]

---

[431] International Crisis Group 2009: 9f., 12f.; United Nations, S/2005/764, 7 December 2005.
[432] International Crisis Group 2006a: 6; United Nations, S/2005/560, 1 September 2006, IX; International Crisis Group 2009b: 1.
[433] International Crisis Group 2005: 3-6; United Nations, S/2005/560, 1 September 2005, II.

Figure 4.19   Election campaign, 2005[434]

---

[434] Global Witness 2005d: 25; BBC 2005.

The first round of elections was held on 11 October 2005 and monitored by 436 international electoral observers. All observer groups – local as well as international – described the elections as "peaceful, orderly, free, fair, transparent and well-administered"[435]. None of the candidates won more than 50 percent of the votes, with the two main candidates, George Weah (28.3 percent) and Ellen Johnson-Sirleaf (19.8 percent), to face off in a second round. In the 8 November runoff, Ellen Johnson-Sirleaf won the presidency with 59.4 percent to George Weah's 40.6 percent. With the releasing of election results, George Weah's party, the Congress for Democratic Change (CDC), alleged fraud during the runoff election and filed a formal complaint on 10 November. It created some tension in Monrovia, with Weah's supporters marching to UNMIL headquarters, the ECOWAS office as well as the Nigerian and U.S. embassies, calling for a rerun of the election. The NEC made its ruling on 16 December, rejecting the CDC claim by asserting that minor technical errors during the run-off election were not wilfully committed. On 21 December, Weah announced the CDC had dropped its case as it was the party's desire to see the Liberian people achieve durable and genuine peace. Although Weah lost the presidency, his CDC party performed well in the legislative elections, winning more seats (15) in the House of Representatives than any other party. In comparison, the Unity Party (UP) of Johnson-Sirleaf won only 8 seats in the House. As her party did not win enough votes to dominate either the Senate or House, Johnson-Sirleaf was to make deals and form coalitions to advance her agenda.[436]

Ellen Johnson-Sirleaf was sworn into office as president of the Liberian republic on 16 January 2006. In her inauguration speech, President Johnson-Sirleaf outlined the main priorities of her administration, including national reconciliation, political inclusion, sustained development and economic administrative reforms.[437] Peace implementation of Accra can be classified as "success" as the four sub-goals of top priority were implemented during the transition phase. The partial implementation of the

[435] United Nations, S/2005/764, 7 December 2005, II.
[436] International Crisis Group 2006a: 1-4; United Nations, S/2005/764, 7 December 2005, II.
[437] United Nations, S/2006/159, 14 March 2006, II.

sub-goals "reintegration" and "reforms" further presented favourable conditions for the transition from peace implementation to peace consolidation. Only the dimension "trade in natural resources" was not addressed during the transition phase.

Figure 4.20   Ellen Johnson-Sirleaf[438]

Summary

The Accra Agreement of 2003 received an unprecedented high international commitment and assistance with the establishment of a 15,000-strong United Nations Mission for Liberia. UNMIL's comprehensive mandate enabled the tackling of various intrusive tasks ranging from the process of disarmament, demobilization, reintegration and rehabilitation, to the reform of the security, judicial and governance sectors. The beginning of the implementation phase had been hampered by political tensions within the transitional government, and the delayed deployment of UN peacekeepers and financial assistance for DDRR. The dynamic, however, changed with the arrival of adequate

---

[438] BBC 2010.

international assistance from the year 2004 onwards. Significant progress was achieved in three crucial areas. First, the security situation improved with the intervention force attaining full troop strength and deploying to all parts of the country. Disarmament and demobilization were successfully completed by late 2004. The training of the new police progressed, and from mid-2006, the new restructured and trained Liberian security forces took up a greater responsibility in national security. Financial shortfalls, however, were responsible for the delay in the provision of reintegration possibilities, the restructuring of the AFL and the dismal conditions in prisons. Secondly, an anti-corruption wave, emanating from civil society, yielded to the suspension and trial of members of the transition government on grounds of embezzlement. The apparent unwillingness on the side of the transitional government to institute essential governance reforms and the high level of embezzlement rampant in the ministries, moreover, led to the introduction of far-reaching measures for the reform of the governance, and the extension of the comprehensive sanctions imposed on Taylor's regime. Thirdly, the conditions for legitimate elections were set up, for example, the reform of the electoral commission, the repatriation of refugees and internally displaced persons, and the registration of voters. The elections proceeded without any major difficulties, and Ellen Johnson-Sirleaf won the presidency in the second run-off against George Weah.

Summary of Case Study

The study of the peace implementation process in Liberia substantiates the hypothesis that the success or failure of peace implementation in the context of a new war is influenced by the respective value of the nature of the conflict, quality of the peace agreement design, and international interest and commitment as the conflict parties determine their preferred course of action under these present conditions.

The peace implementation phase I exemplified that with a low quality of the peace agreement design and medium international commitment, the resolution of a conflict with a difficult conflict nature cannot be achieved. The lack of adequate international support hampered ECOMOG's efforts in implementing the peace agreement, and attacks of peacekeepers by Liberia's factions eventually forced ECOMOG and UN observers to withdraw to Monrovia. Lack of commitment by the factions to the peace process, exemplified by deadlock in the new transitional government and the factions' holding on to conquered areas and natural resources abounding in these areas, brought peace implementation to a standstill. The peace process eventually collapsed with the emergence of new and splinter factions, increasing the fighting in the interior of the country.

The implementation of Abuja I was under the same constraints that had hampered Cotonou due to ECOMOG's financial, logistical and personnel shortcomings and the persistent cease-fire violations. In comparison, the peace implementation phase II with regard to Abuja II experienced a higher quality of the peace agreement design and a greater international interest and commitment. Logistical and financial assistance accorded to ECOMOG enabled the peacekeepers to deploy for the first time throughout the country and launch the disarmament and demobilization process on schedule. The harmonization of relations between ECOWAS member states and between Nigeria and Charles Taylor also helped in keeping the peace process on course amidst political differences between the warring parties. The transition phase was successfully completed with the holding of elections, according the presidency to Charles Taylor. The peace implementation phase II, however, had an essential flaw as it did not prepare for the setting in of the consolidation phase: the reintegration of ex-combatants, the reform of the governance, security and judicial sectors and the regulation of the trade in natural resources was left to the regime of Charles Taylor, which, on the contrary, instituted only changes that benefited its own interests and plunged the country into more debt and misery.

With high manifestations of the quality of the peace agreement design and international interest and commitment, the difficult nature of the conflict with respect to peace implementation phase III could adequately be approached. The deployment of a strong UN mission to Liberia with comprehensive mandate, personnel and resources led to the implementation of the most important sub-goals disarmament, demobilization, power sharing/political participation and elections. Attempts by recalcitrant warring faction' representatives to block reforms in the transitional government were countered by the imposition of far-reaching governance measures by donors and diplomatic communities. In comparison to Abuja II, the peace process did not stop with the holding of elections: mid- to long-term peace consolidating measures (for example, the formation of a new national army and the reform of state revenue management) were introduced during the transition phase, which were to continue into the term of the elected government owing to the long-term international commitment to Liberia's reconstruction. The groundwork for lasting stability was therefore laid through the overhauling of Liberia's state institutions, which had theretofore not served the interest of the Liberian population.

Since the end of the second civil war and the inauguration of the new government in early 2006, Liberia has become more stable and made significant progress in many areas but its peace remains fragile due to the extent of war-related destruction in the political, economical and social sectors. The Fund for Peace notes that the challenges confronting the elected government are enormous and institutional capacity remains weak.[439] Despite the implementation of the Governance and Economic Management Assistance Program (GEMAP) in order to ensure the efficient and transparent use of revenues, corruption continues to be a challenge for the incumbent regime, implicating many high-level officials. Meanwhile, Liberia's economy reached a growth rate of 9.4% in 2008, with a GDP of U.S. $1.34 billion. Since the lifting of sanctions on diamonds and timber, exports of these commodities also contribute to the economic growth. While foreign investments improved, especially in the mining, forestry and rubber industries, much of the population remains impoverished: "Approximately 80% of the population lives below the poverty line, 35% of the population is estimated to be undernourished, and only 15% of the population is estimated to

---

[439] The Fund for Peace: 2.

be employed in the formal economy"[440]. There is no public supply of electricity or running water in the country, and institutions, basic infrastructure, health facilities and the education system remain in bad condition. Despite the continued assistance of UNMIL peacekeepers and UNPOL officers in providing security, reports of police officers being involved in harassment and intimidation of individuals, mob violence and vigilante justice are rampant in the country. The judiciary and the civil service continue to suffer from corruption, limited efficiency and financial shortfall. The future of Liberia, according to The Fund for Peace, thus "largely depends on sustaining the peace and rebuilding the institutions and basic infrastructure that were destroyed during the civil war"[441].

---

[440] The Fund for Peace: 1.
[441] ibid: 2.

Analysis of Research

The theory model contributes to the concretization and explanation of the concepts of new war and peace implementation. First, the broadly phrased assumptions of the new war concept are concretized in this study by considering the characteristics of new wars in the design of the actor and structure levels and revealing the mechanisms presiding between them. The selected context factors describe, for example, the new war-specific framework conditions, which present opportunities and constraints for the various actors and thereby influence their course of action. Secondly, the work contributes to an understanding of the challenges and conditions for success for civil war termination in the implementation phase. The study further makes a contribution to delineating the two phases peace implementation and peace consolidation and explaining success or failure of a peace process in the implementation phase. The generated theoretical model highlights the factors which are decisive or necessary for a successful peace implementation in the context of a new war, whereby the choice of variables and operationalization as well as the preferences and expectations of the actors are tailored to the phase of peace implementation. On the account of given structures and conditions, which have an effect on the actors actively involved in the conflict, the generated theory model can explain peace implementation in a new war, why peace implementation is successful in a particular case and fails in another. The given context factors and conditions provide opportunities and constraints for actions of conflict parties. Under these conditions, the utility maximizing actors choose the course of action most beneficial to their ends: the conflict parties cooperate in respect to peace implementation when their fears are reduced through guarantees and commitment by third parties and their political and financial interests are also secured during peace implementation. Peace implementation is accordingly successful in this instance. By contrast, peace implementation fails and leads to a relapse of large-scale violence when these incentives and commitments are not provided and the interests of the conflict parties are not guaranteed during peace times.

Scope and Limits of Validity

The theory model attempts to explain any peace implementation in a new war through the in-built variance of the dependent and independent variables. The objective is to be able to explain peace implementation in its different outcomes (successful up to failed) in the context of a new war. The study, however, cannot lay claim to be theoretically generalisable for any type of war as the focus is on the explanation of a new war and only the characteristics of this war type are essentially considered here. Additionally, the phase of peace consolidation is omitted through the sole consideration of short-term peace implementing strategies and measures. Peace implementation only deals with the immediate consequences of warfare (for example, the disarmament and demobilization of combatants), while, by contrast, peace consolidation treats the root causes of the war. Especially in the context of a failed state, the process of state-building cannot be left to the affected country's own devices as it does not have the capacity (or willingness on the side of some rulers) to reverse this process on its own accord. Only an active, adequate long-term commitment of third parties can assist the country in getting back on its feet by dealing with the root causes that lead to state failure and civil war in the first place. The Liberian case study exemplified this point: the peace implementation phase II with regards to Abuja II was classified as "success". However, the failure to institute peace consolidating measures, and the lack of timely international pressure on the regime of Taylor and commitment to the stabilization of the country led to the development of a second civil war. A further limit of the study is that the theory model was not subjected to a theory test: the Liberian case study with its three points of analysis formed the last part of the study as a means of illustrating the generated theory model. Essentially, the validity of the theory model cannot be solely determined through the application to only one case study. It requires further applications, which might lead to a substantiation or refinement of the model.

Outlook

A future work could apply the theory model to further peace implementation processes occurring in different countries as well as several points of analysis within one country. In the selection of future case studies, attempt should be made to include new war cases outside West Africa: the Liberian case study could very well exemplify the theory model. As the Liberian civil wars were highly connected to the regional instability and civil wars in its neighbouring states, the same dynamics highlighted for Liberia were at play in Sierra Leone and Côte d'Ivoire. The analysis of Sierra Leone and Côte d'Ivoire using this theory model would thus not lead to a further substantiation of the presented hypotheses. According to this study, the concept of new wars is not considered as restrictive to wars that occurred after the end of the cold war as the features of new wars could already be found in wars before 1989. The privatization and transnationalisation of violence, the emergence of economic motives and criminalization of the economy, as well as the brutalization of war strategies were not new phenomena but were rather given more impetus with the discontinuation of assistance of super powers to client states or factions. Natural resources are generally considered the main financial sources for warfare in new wars, providing the predominant motive for warfare. They are, however, not the only means of finance for warring factions, as illustrated by the military support accorded to Liberia's warring factions by various states. Potential cases for future work could thus include Bosnia, Sudan, Cambodia, Angola, the Democratic Republic of Congo and Afghanistan. Moreover, the theory model could be modified in encompassing not only the peace implementation phase but also peace consolidation, which could, in particular, affect the selection of sub-goals considered as important: the implementation of dimensions such as reforms, reintegration and trade in natural resources would form potential requisites for the success of peace consolidation.

Bibliography

Aboagye, Festus/Bah, Alhaji M. S. (eds.) 2005: A Tortuous Road to Peace: The Dynamics of Regional, UN and International Humanitarian Interventions in Liberia, Pretoria: Institute for Security Studies.

Accord 1996: The Liberian Peace Process 1990-1996, Issue 1 (1996) London: Conciliation Resources. <http://www.c-r.org/our-work/accord/pdfs/down loads.php> Rev. 2010-02-23.

Adebajo, Adekeye 2002a: Building Peace in West Africa: Liberia, Sierra Leone, and Guinea-Bissau, London, Boulder: Lynne Rienner Publishers.

Adebajo, Adekeye 2002b: Liberia's Civil War: Nigeria, ECOMOG, and Regional Security in West Africa, London, Boulder: Lynne Rienner Publishers.

Adebajo, Adekeye/Rashid, Ismail (eds.) 2004: West Africa's Security Challenges: Building Peace in a Troubled Region, Boulder, London: Lynne Rienner Publishers.

Alao, Abiodun/Mackinlay, John 1995: Liberia 1994: ECOMOG and UNOMIL Response to a Complex Emergency, Occasional Paper Series 2. <http://www.unu.edu/unupress/ops2.html> Rev. 2010-05-13.

Alao, Abiodun/Mackinlay, John/Olonisakin, Funmi 1999: Peacekeepers, Politicians, and Warlords: The Liberian Peace Process, Tokyo, NY, Paris: United Nations University Press.

Ballentine, Karen/Sherman, Jake 2003: The Political Economy of Armed Conflict: Beyond Greed and Grievance, Boulder, London: Lynne Rienner Publishers.

Ballentine, Karen/Nitzschke, Heiko 2005: Profiting from Peace: Managing the Resource Dimensions of Civil War, Boulder, London: Lynne Rienner Publishers.

Banks, Michael 1987: Four Conceptions of Peace, in: Sandole, Dennis J. D./Sandole-Staroste, Ingrid (eds.): Conflict Management and Problem Solving: Interpersonal to International Applications, London: Frances Pinter Publishers, 259-274.

Basedau, Matthias/Mehler, Andreas (eds.) 2005: Resource Politics in Sub-Saharan Africa, Hamburg African Studies 14, Hamburg: Institut für Afrika-Kunde.

Bayol, Nicholas/Chevalier, Jean-Francois 2004: Current State of the Forest Cover in Liberia, Appendix 3 – Land cover map, World Bank. <http://www.fao.org/forestry/lfi/ 29026/en/> Rev. 2010-02-23.

BBC 2000: Diamonds: A Rebel's Best Friend. <http://news.bbc.co.uk/2/hi/africa/745194.stm> Rev. 2010-05-12.

BBC 2002: Humanitarian Crisis Looms in Liberia. <http://news.bbc.co.uk/2/hi/africa/1813866.stm> Rev. 2010-05-13.

BBC 2003a: Liberia: The Aid Agencies. <http://news.bbc.co.uk/2/hi/programmes/hardtalk/3132813.stm> 2010-05-12.

BBC 2003b: In Pictures: Liberia Peacekeepers. <http://news.bbc.co.uk/2/hi/in_depth/photo_gallery/3133693.stm> Rev. 2010-05-13.

BBC 2003c: In Pictures: Desperate Liberia. <http://news.bbc.co.uk/2/hi/in_depth/photo_gallery/3113005.stm> Rev. 2010-05-13.

BBC 2003d: In Pictures: Tough Week for Monrovia. <http://news.bbc.co.uk/2/hi/in_depth/photo_gallery/2988332.stm> Rev. 2010-05-13.

BBC 2005: Focus Shifts to Liberia's Recovery. <http://news.bbc.co.uk/2/hi/africa/4284642.stm> Rev. 2010-05-13.

BBC 2009a: Timeline: Liberia. <http://news.bbc.co.uk/2/hi/africa/country_profiles/1043567.stm> 2010-05-12.

BBC 2009b: African View: Memoirs of Taylor. <http://news.bbc.co.uk/2/hi/africa/8171244.stm> Rev. 2010-05-12.

BBC 2010: Liberia Country Profile. <http://news.bbc.co.uk/2/hi/africa/country_profiles/1043500.stm#facts> Rev. 2010-05-13.

Berdal, Mats 2003: How "New" are "New Wars"? Global Economic Change and the Study of Civil War, in: Global Governance 9, 477-502.

Bonacker, Thorsten/Imbusch, Peter 2006: Zentrale Begriffe der Friedens- und Konfliktforschung: Konflikt, Gewalt, Krieg, Frieden, in: Imbusch, Peter/Zoll, Ralf (eds.): Friedens- und Konfliktforschung: Eine Einführung, 4th revised edition, Wiesbaden: VS Verlag für Sozialwissenschaften, 67-142.

Brock, Lothar 1990: "Frieden": Überlegungen zur Theoriebildung, in: Rittberger, Volker (ed.): Theorien der Internationalen Beziehungen: Bestandsaufnahme und Forschungsperspektiven, Opladen, 71-89.

Brzoska, Michael (ed.) 2001: Smart Sanctions: The Next Steps, Baden-Baden: Nomos Verlagsgesellschaft.

Brzoska, Michael/Paes, Wolf-Christian 2007: Die Rolle externer wirtschaftlicher Akteure in Bürgerkriegsökonomien und ihre Bedeutung für Kriegsbeendigungs-strategien in Afrika südlich der Sahara, Osnabrück: Deutsche Stiftung Friedensforschung (DSF).

Chojnacki, Sven 2004: Wandel der Kriegsformen – Ein kritischer Literaturbericht, in: Leviathan 32:3, 402-424.

Chojnacki, Sven 2006: Kriege im Wandel: Eine typologische und empirische Bestandsaufnahme, in: Geis, Anna (ed.): Den Krieg überdenken: Kriegsbegriffe und Kriegstheorien in der Kontroverse, Baden-Baden: Nomos Verlagsgesellschaft, 47-74.

Chojnacki, Sven/Reisch, Gregor 2008a: New List of Wars, 1946-2006, Version 1.3 (January 2008), FU Berlin, Berliner Forschungsgruppe Krieg.

Chojnacki, Sven/Reisch, Gregor 2008b: Perspectives on War: Collecting, Comparing and Disaggregating Data on Violent Conflicts, Research Center SFB 700 Governance in Areas of Limited Statehood, FU Berlin, in: S+F (26th Vol.) 4/2008.

CNN 1997a: Liberian Election Ends Without Violence. <http://www.cnn.com/ WORLD/9707/19/liberia/index.html> Rev. 2010-05-13.

CNN 1997b: Election First Step in Rebuilding Shattered Liberia. <http://www.cnn.com/WORLD/9707/17/liberia/index.html> Rev. 2010-05-13.

CNN 1997c: Liberian Warlord Gets Off Warpath, Onto Campaign Trail. <http://www.cnn.com/WORLD/9702/27/liberia.last/index.html?iref=allsearch > Rev. 2010-05-13.

CNN 1997d: U.S., W. Africa Join Forces to Aid Liberian Elections. <http:// www.cnn.com/WORLD/9702/25/liberia.us/ind ex.html> Rev. 2010-05-13.

Collier, Paul/Elliott, V. L./Hegre, Havard/Hoeffler, Anke/Reynal-Querol, Marta/Sambanis, Nicholas 2003: Breaking the Conflict Trap: Civil War and Development Policy, A World Bank Policy Research Report, World Bank, Oxford University Press. <http://www.worldbank.org> Rev. 2007-02-07.

Van Creveld, Martin 1991: The Transformation of War, New York: The Free Press.

Darby, John/Mac Ginty, Roger (eds.) 2003: Contemporary Peacemaking: Conflict, Violence and Peace Processes, Basingstoke, NY: Palgrave Macmillan.

Debiel, Tobias 1996: Kriegswirtschaft und Friedenskonsolidierung, INEF Report Duisburg, Issue 20/1996.

Doyle, Michael/Sambanis, Nicholas 2000: International Peacebuilding: A Theoretical and Quantitative Analysis, in: American Political Science Review 94:4, 779-801.

Doyle, Michael/Sambanis, Nicholas 2006: Making War and Building Peace, Princeton, Oxford: Princeton University Press.

Duffield, Mark 2000: Globalization, Transborder Trade, and War Economies, in: Berdal, Mats/Malone, David M.: Greed and Grievance: Economic Agendas in Civil Wars, Boulder: Rienner, 69-90.

ECOWAS 1978: Protocol on Non-Aggression. <http://www.iss.co.za/AF/RegOrg/unity_to_Union/pdfs/ecowas/14ProtNonAggre.pdf> Rev. 2009-10-29.

ECOWAS 1981: Protocol Relating to Mutual Assistance of Defence. <http://www.iss.co.za/af/regorg/unity_to_union/pdfs/ecowas/13ProtMutualDef Ass.pdf> Rev. 2009-10-29.

ECOWAS 1999: Protocol Relating to the Mechanism for Conflict Prevention, Management, Resolution, Peace-keeping and Security. <http://www.sec.ecowas.int/sitecedeao/english/ap10129 9.htm> Rev. 2009-10-29.

Evans, Gareth/Sahnoun, Mohamed 2001: The Responsibility to Protect, Report of the International Commission on Intervention and State Sovereignty, Ottawa. <http://www.iciss.ca/pdf/ commission-report.pdf> Rev. 2008-02-19.

Van Evera, Stephen 1997: Guide to Methods for Students of Political Science, Ithaca, NY: Cornell University Press.

Fearon, James D. 2004: Why Do Some Civil Wars Last So Much Longer Than Others?, in: Journal of Peace Research 41:3, 275-301.

Ferdowski, Mir A./Matthies, Volker (eds.) 2003: Den Frieden gewinnen: Zur Konsolidierung von Friedensprozessen in Nachkriegsgesellschaften, Bonn: Dietz.

Fortna, Virginia Page 2004: Peace Time: Cease-Fire Agreements and the Durability of Peace, Princeton: Princeton University Press, 1-38.

Frey, Bruno S. 2008: Terrorism from the Rational Choice Point of View, in: Diekmann, Andreas/Eichner, Klaus/Schmidt, Peter/Voss, Thomas (eds.): Rational Choice: Theoretische Analysen und empirische Resultate, Wiesbaden: VS Verlag für Sozialwissenschaften, 211-222.

Galtung, Johan 1975: Strukturelle Gewalt: Beiträge zur Friedens- und Konfliktforschung, Reinbek: Rowohlt, 7-36.

Galtung, Johan 1996: Peace by Peaceful Means: Peace and Conflict, Development and Civilization, International Peace Research Institute, Oslo; London, Thousand Oaks, New Delhi: Sage Publications.

Gleditsch, Nils Petter/Wallensteen, Peter/Eriksson, Mikael/Sollenberg, Margareta/Strand, Havard 2002: Armed Conflict 1946-2001: A New Dataset, in: Journal of Peace Research 39:5, 615-637.

Gleditsch, Nils Petter/Wallensteen, Peter/Eriksson, Mikael/Sollenberg, Margareta/Strand, Havard 2006: Armed Conflict 1946-2005: Conflict List 1946-2005. <http://www.udcp.uu.se/research/UCDP/our_data1.htm> Rev. 2006-12-19.

Global Witness 2001a: Global witness calls on UN Security Council to embargo Liberian "Logs of war", Press Release 17/01/2001. <http://www.globalwitness.org/media_library_detail.php/299/en/global_witne ss_calls_on_un_security_council_to_emb> Rev. 2009-10-29.

Global Witness 2001b: Liberian timber profits finance regional conflict, Press Release 04/05/2001. <http://www.globalwitness.org/media_library_detail.php /245/en/liberian_timber_profits_finance_regional_conflict> Rev. 2009-10-29.

Global Witness 2001c: Liberia breaches UN Sanctions – whilst its logging industry funds arms imports and RUF rebels, Press Release 06/09/2001. <http://www.globalwitness.org/media_library_detail.php/246/en/liberia_breac hes_un_sanctions_whilst_its_logging_i> Rev. 2009-10-29.

Global Witness 2001d: Taylor-Made: The Pivotal Role of Liberia's Forests and Flag of Convenience in Regional Conflict, Report 07/09/2001. <http://www.globalwitness.org/media_library _detail.php/97/en/taylor_made> Rev. 2009-10-29.

Global Witness 2002a: Briefing Document: Liberia's Logs of War: Underpinning Conflict, Press Release 03/05/2002. <http://www.global witness.org/media_library_detail.php/255/en/briefing_document_liberias_logs _of_war_underpinnin> Rev. 2009-10-29.

Global Witness 2002b: The Logs of War: The Timber Trade and Armed Conflict, Report 01/03/2002. <http://www.globalwitness.org/media _library _detail.php/89/en/the_logs_of_war> Rev. 2009-10-29.

Global Witness 2003a: West African arms trafficking and mercenary activities supported by the Liberian government and logging companies, Press Release 31/03/2003. <http://www.globalwitness.org/media_library_detail.php/289/en/ west_african_arms_trafficking_and_mercenary_activi> Rev. 2009-10-29.

Global Witness 2003b: Briefing Document: Recommendations and situational update presented to the UN Security Council, Press Release 20/06/2003. <http://www.globalwitness.org/media_library_detail.php/305/en/briefing_doc ument_recommendations_and_situational_> Rev. 2009-10-29.

Global Witness 2003c: Global Witness Briefing Document – Liberia: Lifting Sanctions will fuel instability and jeopardise peace, Press Release 04/09/2003. <http://www.globalwitness.org/media_library_detail.php/312/en/global_witne ss_briefing_document_liberia_lifting_s> Rev. 2009-10-29.

Global Witness 2003d: The Usual Suspects: Liberia's Weapons and Mercenaries in Côte d'Ivoire and Sierra Leone, Report 31/03/2003. <http://www.globalwitness.org/media_library_detail.php/96/en/the_usual_sus pects> Rev. 2009-10-29.

Global Witness 2004a: Liberia: Resource – Curse or Cure, Report 14/09/2004. <http://www.globalwitness.org/media_library_detail.php/122/en/resource_curs e_or_cure> Rev. 2009-10-29.

Global Witness 2004b: Dangerous Liaisons: The continued relationship between Liberia's natural resource industries, arms trafficking and regional insecurity, Report 08/12/2004. <http://www.globalwitness.org/media_library_ detail.php/128/en/dangerous _liaisons> Rev. 2009-10-29.

Global Witness 2005a: Critical shortfall in funding and lack of reform threaten to undermine stability in Liberia, Press Release 09/02/2005. <http://www.globalwitness.org/media_library_detail.php/366/en/critical_short fall_in_funding_and_lack_of_reform_t> Rev. 2009-10-29.

Global Witness 2005b: Liberia: Uncontrolled Liberian resource exploitation and manipulation by Charles Taylor continue to threaten peace in West Africa, Press Release 15/06/2005. <http://www.globalwitness.org/media_library_detai l.php/380/en/liberia_uncontrolled_liberian_resource_exploitatio> Rev. 2009-10-29.

Global Witness 2005c: Global Witness welcomes the report of the Forest Concession Review Committee and urges the Liberian government to sign and implement its recommendations, Press Release 29/07/2005. <http://www.globalwitness.org/media_library_detail.php/389/en/global_witne ss_welcomes_the_report_of_the_forest_c> Rev. 2009-10-29.

Global Witness 2005d: An Architecture of Instability: How the critical link between natural resources and conflict remains unbroken, Policy briefing 12/2005. <http://www.globalwitness.org/media_library_detail.php/144/en/an_ architecture_of_instability> Rev. 2010-05-11.

Global Witness 2006a: Global Witness welcomes President Sirleaf's decision to cancel all forest concession agreements, Press Release 09/02/2006. <http://www.globalwitness.org/media_library_detail.php/421/en/global_witne ss_welcomes_president_sirleafs_decisio> Rev. 2009-10-29.

Global Witness 2006b: Liberian diamonds, timber and rubber still exploited by ex-combatants, Press Release 01/06/2006. <http://www.globalwitness.org/ media_library_detail.php/441/en/liberian_diamonds_timber_and_rubber_still_ exploite> Rev. 2009-10-29.

Global Witness 2006c: United Nations Security Council lifts Liberia timber sanctions despite insufficient reform of the industry, Press Release 22/06/2006. <http://www.globalwitness.org/media_library_detail.php/448/en/united_nation s_security_council_lifts_liberia_timb> Rev. 2009-10-29.

Global Witness 2006d: Mittal Steel's US$900 million deal in Liberia is inequitable, says new Global Witness report, Press Release 02/10/2006. <http://www.globalwitness.org/media_library_detail.php/459/en/mittal_steels_ us900_million_deal_in_liberia_is_ine> Rev. 2009-10-29.

Global Witness 2006e: Cautiously Optimistic: The Case for Maintaining Sanctions in Liberia, Briefing Document 06/2006. <http://www.global witness.org/media_library_detail.php/142/en/cautiously_optimistic_the_case_f or_maintaining_san> Rev. 2010-05-13.

Greenpeace 2001: The Relationship Between the Timber Sector, Arms Trafficking and the Destruction of the Forests in Liberia, <http://www.greenpeace.es> Rev. 2010-02-22.

Habermas, Jürgen 1998: Die postnationale Konstellation und die Zukunft der Demokratie, in: Blätter für deutsche und internationale Politik 7/98, 804-817.

Hadden, R. Lee 2006: The Geology of Liberia: A Selected Bibliography of Liberian Geology, Geography and Earth Science, <http://www.dtic.mil/cgi-bin/GetTRDoc?AD=ADA451649&Loc ation=U2&doc=GetTRDoc.pdf> Rev. 2010-02-22.

Hammermaster, E. T. 1985: Assistance to the Forestry Development Authority of Liberia: Forest Resources Mapping of Liberia, Food and Agriculture Organisation of the United Nations, Trust Fund Project UTF/LIR/008/LIR. <ftp://ftp.fao.org/ docrep/fao/field/007/ae662e/ae662e.pdf> Rev. 2010-05-11.

Hampson, Fen Osler 1996: Nurturing Peace: Why Peace Settlements Succeed or Fail, Washington, DC: United States Institute of Peace Press.

Hampson, Fen Osler 2001: Parent, Midwife, or Accidential Executioner? The Role of Third Parties in Ending Violent Conflict, in: Crocker, Chester/Hampson, Fen Osler/Aall, Pamela (eds.): Turbulent Peace: The Challenges of Managing International Conflict, Washington, DC: United States Institute of Peace Press, 387-406.

Hartzell, Caroline/Hoddie, Matthew/Rothchild, Daniel 2001: Stabilizing the Peace After Civil War: An Investigation of Some Key Variables, in: International Organization 55:1, 183-208.

Hartzell, Caroline/Hoddie, Matthew 2003: Institutionalizing Peace: Power Sharing and Post-Civil War Conflict Management, in: American Journal of Political Science 47:2, 318-333.

Hegre, Havard 2004: The Duration and Termination of Civil War, in: Journal of Peace Research 41:3, 243-252.

Held, David/McGrew, Anthony/Goldblatt, David/Perraten, Jonathan 1999: Global Transformations: Politics, Economics and Culture, Cambridge: Polity Press, 1-28, 424-444.

Heupel, Monica/Zangl, Bernhard 2004: Von "alten" und "neuen" Kriegen – Zum Gestaltwandel kriegerischer Gewalt, in: Politische Vierteljahresschrift 45:3, 346-369.

Heupel, Monica 2005: Friedenskonsolidierung im Zeitalter der "neuen" Kriege: Der Wandel der Gewaltökonomien als Herausforderung, Wiesbaden: VS Verlag für Sozial-wissenschaften.

Hofmeier, Rolf/Mehler, Andreas (eds.) 2004: Kleines Afrika-Lexikon: Politik – Wirtschaft – Kultur, Bundeszentrale für politische Bildung, München: Verlag C.H. Beck oHG.

International Crisis Group: Liberia, <http://www.crisisgroup.org/home/index.cfm?id= 1237&l=1> Rev. 2009-12-08.

International Crisis Group 2002a: Liberia: The Key to Ending Regional Instability, ICG Africa Report No. 43, 24/04/2002. <http://www.crisis group.org/home/index.cfm?id=1533&l=1> Rev. 2009-10-29.

International Crisis Group 2002b: Liberia: Unravelling, ICG Africa Briefing Paper, 19/08/2002, <http://www.crisisgroup.org/library/documents/report_archive/A400741_1 9082002.pdf> Rev. 2010-04-16.

International Crisis Group 2003a: Tackling Liberia: The Eye of the Regional Storm, ICG Africa Report No. 62, 30/04/2003, <http://www.crisisgroup.org/library/documents/report_archive/A400960_30042003.pdf> Rev. 2010-04-16.

International Crisis Group 2003b: Liberia: Security Challenges, ICG Africa Report No. 71, 03/11/2003. <http://www.crisisgroup.org/home/index.cfm?id=2344&l=1> Rev. 2009-10-29.

International Crisis Group 2004a: Rebuilding Liberia: Prospects and Perils, ICG Africa Report No. 75, 30/01/2004. <http://www.crisisgroup.org/home/index.cfm?id=2496&l=1> Rev. 2009-10-29.

International Crisis Group 2004b: Liberia and Sierra Leone: Rebuilding Failed States, Crisis Group Africa Report N°87, 08/12/2004. <http://www.crisisgroup.org/home/index.cfm?id=31 56&l=1> Rev. 2009-10-29.

International Crisis Group 2005: Liberia's Elections: Necessary But Not Sufficient, Africa Report N°98, 07/09/2005. <http://www.crisisgroup.org/home/index.cfm?id=3646&l=1> Rev. 2009-10-29.

International Crisis Group 2006a: Liberia: Staying Focused, Crisis Group Africa Briefing N°36, 13/01/2006. <http://www.crisisgroup.org/~/media/Files/africa/west-africa/liberia/B036%20Liberia%20Staying%20Focused.ashx> Rev. 2010-05-02.

International Crisis Group 2006b: Liberia: Resurrecting the Justice System, Africa Report N°107, 06/04/2006. <http://www.crisisgroup.org/home/index.cfm?id=4061&l=1> Rev. 2009-10-29.

International Crisis Group 2009: Liberia: Uneven Progress in Security Sector Reform, Africa Report N°148, 13/01/2009. <http://www.crisisgroup.org/home/index.cfm?id=5867&l=1> Rev. 2009-10-29.

Johnson-Sirleaf, Ellen 2007: Annual Message by Her Excellency Ellen Johnson-Sirleaf – President of the Republic of Liberia, Delivered to the 52nd Legislature of the Republic of Liberia, Virginia, Liberia, 29th January 2007.

Jung, Dietrich (ed.) 2003: Shadow Globalization, Ethnic Conflicts and New Wars: A Political Economy of Intra-State War, London, New York: Routledge.

Kaldor, Mary 1999: New and Old Wars: Organized Violence in a Global Era, Cambridge.

Kamara, Abdul Rahman 2002: ECOMOG, A Sub-Regional Instrument for Conflict Resolution: The 1990-97 ECOWAS-Liberia Peace Process, Dissertation, University of Bradford, September 2002.

King, Charles 1997: Ending Civil Wars, Adelphi Paper 308, International Institute for Strategic Studies, Oxford: Oxford University Press.

Körner, Peter 1996: Macht- und Interessenpolitik in der ECOWAS-Region und der Krieg in Liberia: Die politische Dimension regionaler Integration in Westafrika, Hamburg: Institut für Afrika-Kunde.

Korte, Werner 1997: Prozesse des Staatszerfalls in Liberia, in: WeltTrends 14, Spring 1997, 55-80.

Krumwiede, Heinrich-W./Waldmann, Peter (eds.) 1998: Bürgerkriege: Folgen und Regulierungsmöglichkeiten, Baden-Baden: Nomos Verlag.

Kunz, Volker 2004: Rational Choice, Frankfurt, New York: Campus Verlag.

Levitt, Jeremy I. 2005: The Evolution of Deadly Conflict in Liberia: From 'Paternaltarianism' to State Collapse, Durham, North Carolina: Carolina Academic Press.

Licklider, Roy (ed.) 1993: Stopping the Killing: How Civil Wars End, New York.

Licklider, Roy 2001: Obstacles to Peace Settlements, in: Crocker, Chester/Hampson, Fen Osler/Aall, Pamela (eds.): Turbulent Peace: The Challenges of Managing International Conflict, Washington, DC: United States Institute of Peace Press, 697-718.

Linklater Andrew (ed.) 2000: International Relations: Critical Concepts in Political Science, London, New York: Routledge, 324-333.

Little, Daniel 1991: Varieties of Social Explanation: An Introduction to the Philosophy of Social Science, Boulder, San Francisco, Oxford: Westview Press, 1-38.

Lowenkopf, Martin 1995: Liberia: Putting the State Back Together, in: Zartman, William I. (ed.): Collapsed States: The Disintegration and Restoration of Legitimate Authority, Boulder, London: Lynne Rienner Publishers, 91-108.

Lujala, Päivi 2003: Classification of Natural Resources, <http://www.essex.ac. uk/ECPR/events/jointsessions/paperarchive/edinburgh/ws9/Lujala.pdf> Rev. 2010-02-21.

MacQueen, Norrie 2006: Peacekeeping and the International System, Abingdon: Routledge.

Magyar, Karl P. 1998: Peacekeeping in Africa: ECOMOG in Liberia, London, NY: Macmillan Press/St. Martin's Press.

Mair, Stefan 2000: Regionale Integration und Kooperation in Afrika südlich der Sahara, Ebenhausen: Stiftung Wissenschaft und Politik.

Matthies, Volker (ed.) 1995: Vom Krieg zum Frieden: Kriegsbeendigung und Friedenskonsolidierung, Bremen: Ed. Temmen.

Matthies, Volker 2004: Der vernachlässigte Blick auf den Frieden: Eine Welt voller neuer Kriege?, in: Der Bürger im Staat 54:4, 185-191.

McAnulla, Stuart 2002: Structure and Agency, in: Marsh, David/Stoker, Gerry (eds.): Theory and Methods in Political Science, 2nd rev. ed., Houndsmills, Basingstoke: Palgrave Macmillan, 271-291.

Müller, Harald 2003: Begriff, Theorien und Praxis des Friedens, in: Hellmann, Gunther/Wolf, Klaus Dieter/Zürn, Michael (eds.): Die neuen Internationalen Beziehungen: Forschungsstand und Perspektiven in Deutschland, Baden-Baden: Nomos Verlagsgesellschaft, 209-250.

Münkler, Herfried 2002: Die neuen Kriege, Reinbek: Rowohlt Verlag.

Nation Master: Economy Statistics – GDP – Liberia. <http://www.nationmast er.com/time.php?stat=eco_gdp-economy-gdp&country=li-liberia> Rev. 2009-12-21.

Nitzschke, Heiko 2003: Transforming War Economies: Challenges for Peacemaking and Peacebuilding, 725th Wilton Park Conference, International Peace Academy, New York. <http://www.ipacademy.org/publication/meeting-notes/detail/97-transforming-war-economies-challenges-for-peacemaking-and-peacebuilding.html> Rev. 2008-06-12.

Pleming, Sue/Wroughton, Lesley 2007: US to cancel Liberia debt, urges others to follow, Reuters, 13/02/2007. <http://www.alertnet.org/thenews/newsdesk/N13172609.htm> Rev. 2007-03-19.

Pugh, Michael/Cooper, Neil 2004: War Economies in a Regional Context: Challenges of Transformation, Boulder, London: Lynne Rienner Publishers.

Ramsbotham, Oliver/Woodhouse, Tom/Miall, Hugh 2005: Contemporary Conflict Resolution, 2nd ed., Cambridge, Malden: Polity Press.

Reno, William 1998: Warlord Politics and African States, Boulder, London: Lynne Rinner Publishers.

Reno, William 2004: Reconstructing Peace in Liberia, in: Ali, Taisier M./Matthews, Robert O. (eds.): Durable Peace: Challenges for Peacebuilding in Africa, Toronto, Buffalo, London: University of Toronto Press Inc., 115-141.

Rittberger, Volker 2001a: Realism, in: Rittberger, Volker: Introduction to International Relations, Lecture notes.

Rittberger, Volker 2001b: Rational Institutionalism, in: Rittberger, Volker: Introduction to International Relations, Lecture notes.

Rittberger, Volker/Zangl, Bernhard 2003: Internationale Organisationen – Politik und Geschichte: Europäische und weltweite internationale Zusammenschlüsse, 3rd. ed., Leske + Budrich, Opladen.

Rittberger, Volker 2008a: Einführung in die Thematik: Widersprüchliche Tendenzen der gegenwärtigen Weltpolitik, in: Rittberger, Volker: Grundzüge der Weltpolitik, Lecture notes.

Rittberger, Volker 2008b: Globalisierung und Fragmentierung als weltpolitische makroprozessuale Rahmenbedingungen, in: Rittberger, Volker: Grundzüge der Weltpolitik, Lecture notes.

Roberts, James C.: Anarchy, The Internet Encyclopedia of International Relations, Towson University. <http://wwwnew.towson.edu/polsci/irencyc/anarchy.htm> Rev. 2009-11-11.

Ross, Michael 2004a: What Do We Know About Natural Resources and Civil War?, Journal of Peace Research 41:3, 337-356.

Ross, Michael 2004b: How Do Natural Resources Influence Civil War? Evidence From Thirteen Cases, in: International Organization 58:1, 35-67.

Ruf, Werner (ed.) 2003: Politische Ökonomie der Gewalt: Staatszerfall und die Privatisierung von Gewalt und Krieg, Opladen: Leske + Budrich.

Sambolah, Richard 2005: Report on the Rapid Faunal Surveys of Seven Liberian Forest Areas Under Investigation for Conservation, Fauna & Flora International (FFI) – Liberia.

Schimmelpfennig, Frank 1995: Debatten zwischen Staaten, Opladen, 250-266.

Schlichte, Klaus 2006: Neue Kriege oder alte Thesen? Wirklichkeit und Repräsentation kriegerischer Gewalt in der Politikwissenschaft, in: Geiss, Anna (ed.): Neue Kriegstheorien, Baden-Baden.

Schlichte, Klaus 2008: „Staatszerfall" und die Dilemmata der intervenierenden Demokratie, in: Brodocz, André/Llanque, Marcus/Schaal, Gary S. (eds.): Bedrohungen der Demokratie, Wiesbaden: VS Verlag für Sozialwissenschaften, 136-151.

Scholte, Jan Aart 2005: Globalization: A Critical Introduction, Basingstoke: Palgrave Macmillan, 49-84.

Stedman, Stephen J. 1997: Spoiler Problems in Peace Processes, in: International Security 22:2, 5-33.

Stedman, Stephen J. 2001a: International Implementation of Peace Agreements in Civil Wars: Findings from a Study of Sixteen Cases, in: Crocker, Chester/Hampson, Fen Osler/Aall, Pamela (eds.): Turbulent Peace: The Challenges of Managing International Conflict, Washington, DC: United States Institute of Peace Press, 737-752.

Stedman, Stephen J. 2001b: Implementing Peace Agreements in Civil Wars: Lessons and Recommendations for Policymakers, IPA Policy Paper Series on Peace Implementation, New York, May 2001. <http://www.ipacademy.org/ publication/policy-papers/detail/158-implementing-peace-agreements-in-civil-wars-lessons-and-recommendations-for-policymakers.html> Rev. 2009-10-29.

Stedman, Stephen J./Rothchild, Donald/Cousens, Elizabeth M. (eds.) 2002: Ending Civil Wars: The Implementation of Peace Agreements, Boulder, Colorado: Lynne Rienner Publishers.

The Fund for Peace: Liberia, <http://www.fundforpeace.org/web/ index2.php?option=com_content&task=view&id=239&pop=1&page=0&Itemi d=379> Rev. 2009-12-21.

Thürer, Daniel 1995: Der Wegfall effektiver Staatsgewalt: „The Failed State", in: Thürer, Daniel/Herdegen, Matthias/Hohloch, Gerhard: Der Wegfall effektiver Staatsgewalt: The Failed State, Heidelberg: C.F. Müller Verlag, 9-47.

Toweh, Alphonso 2007a: Liberia's "Iron Lady" ends first year on a high, Reuters, 14/01/2007. <http://www.reuters.com/article/latestCrisis/idUSL 14143930> Rev. 2007-03-19.

Toweh, Alphonso 2007b: Liberia says new Mittal deal worth extra $100 mln, Reuters, 16/01/2007. <http://www.reuters.com/ar ticle/companyNewsAndPR/ idUSL1622651820 070116> Rev. 2007-03-19.

Toweh, Alphonso 2007c: China's Hu visit raises hopes in war-torn Liberia, 01/02/2007. <http://www.reuters.com/article/bondsNews/idUSL0192449920 070201> Rev. 2007-03-19.

United Nations: General Assembly: resolutions: A/RES/45/232, 21/12/1990; A/RES/55/56, 01/12/2000.

United Nations 1992: General Assembly/Security Council, An Agenda for Peace: Preventive Diplomacy, Peacemaking and Peace-keeping 1992, A/47/277-S/24111, 17/06/1992. <http:// www.un.org/Docs/SC/agpeace.html> Rev. 2008-02-19.

United Nations 2000: General Assembly/Security Council, The Brahimi Report, Report of the Panel on United Nations Peace Operations, A/55/305-S/2000/809, 21/08/2000. <http://www.un.org/peace/reports/peace_operations/ docs/a_55_305.pdf> Rev. 2008-02-19.

United Nations: Secretary General: reports: S/22133, 22/01/1991; S/24815, 30/10/1991, Yamoussoukro IV Agreement; S/26272, 25/07/1993, Cotonou Peace Agreement; S/1994/1174, Akosombo Agreement; S/1995/7, Accra Agreement; S/1995/742, 19/08/1995, Abuja Agreement I; S/1996/362, 21/05/1996.

United Nations: Security Council, progress reports of the Secretary-General on the United Nations Mission in Liberia: S/2003/466, 22/04/2003; S/2003/850, 29/08/2003; S/2003/1175, 15/12/2003; S/2004/229, 22/03/2004; S/2004/430, 26/05/2004; S/2004/725, 10/09/2004; S/2004/972, 17/12/2004; S/2005/177, 17/03/2005; S/2005/391, 16/06/2005; S/2005/560, 01/09/2005; S/2005/764, 07/12/2005; S/2006/159, 14/03/2006; S/2006/376, 09/06/2006; S/2006/743,

12/09/2006; S/2006/958, 11/12/2006; S/2007/151, 15/03/2007; S/2007/479, 08/08/2007.

United Nations: Security Council: resolutions: S/RES/788, 19/11/1992; S/RES/813, 26/03/1993; S/RES/856, 10/08/1993; S/RES/866, 22/09/1993; S/RES/911, 21/04/1994; S/RES/950, 21/10/1994; S/RES/985, 13/04/1995; S/RES/1001, 30/06/1995; S/RES/1014, 15/09/1995; S/RES/1020, 10/11/1995; S/RES/1041, 29/01/1996; S/RES/1059, 31/05/1996; S/RES/1071, 30/08/1996; S/RES/1083, 27/11/1996; S/RES/1100, 27/03/1997; S/RES/1116, 27/06/1997; S/RES/1132, 08/10/1997; S/RES/1171, 05/06/1998; S/RES/1209, 19/11/1998; S/RES/1306, 05/07/2000; S/RES/1318, 07/09/2000; S/RES/1343, 07/03/2001; S/RES/1395, 27/02/2002; S/RES/1408, 07/03/2002; S/RES/1458, 28/01/2003; S/RES/1478, 06/05/2003; S/RES/1497, 01/08/2003; S/RES/1509, 19/09/2003; S/RES/1521, 22/12/2003; S/RES/1532, 12/03/2004; S/RES/1549, 17/06/2004; S/RES/1561, 17/09/2004; S/RES/1579, 21/12/2004; S/RES/1607, 21/06/2005; S/RES/1626, 19/09/2005; S/RES/1638, 11/11/2005; S/RES/1647, 20/12/2005; S/RES/1667, 31/03/2006; S/RES/1683, 13/06/2006; S/RES/1689, 20/06/2006; S/RES/1694, 13/07/2006; S/RES/1712, 29/09/2006; S/RES/1753, 27/04/2007.

Uppsala Conflict Data Program 2006a: UCDP/PRIO Armed Conflict Dataset Codebook, Uppsala University. <http://www.pcr.uu.se/publications/UCDP_pub/Codebook_v4-2006b.pdf> Rev. 2006-12-19.

Uppsala Conflict Data Program 2006b: Conflict Database: Definitions, Uppsala University. <http://www.pcr.uu.se/database/definitions_all.htm> Rev. 2006-12-19.

Uppsala Conflict Data Program 2008: Liberia: Detailed Information – Whole Conflict, Uppsala University. <http://www.pcr.uu.se/gpdatabase/gpcountry.php?id=94&regionSelect=2-Southern_Africa#> Rev. 2010-02-19.

USGS Minerals Information: Liberia. <http://minerals.usgs.gov/minerals/pubs/country/maps/92589.gif> Rev. 2010-02-23.

Van Walraven, Klaas 1999: The Pretence of Peace-keeping: ECOMOG, West Africa and Liberia (1990-1998), Netherlands Institute of International Relations Clingendael, Clingendael-Study, The Hague. <http://www.clingendael.nl>

Walter, Barbara 1999: Designing Transitions from Civil War, in: International Security 24:1, 127-155.

Walter, Barbara 2002: Committing to Peace. The Successful Settlement of Civil Wars, Princeton: Princeton University Press, 3-43.

Walter, Barbara 2004: Does Conflict Beget Conflict? Explaining Recurring Civil War, in: Journal of Peace Research 41:3, 371-388.

Wallensteen, Peter 2002: Understanding Conflict Resolution, London: Sage.

Wallensteen, Peter/Staibano, Carina 2005 (eds.): International Sanctions: Between Words and Wars in the Global System, London, New York: Frank Cass.

Wikipedia: Rational Choice Theory, 2. <http://en.wikipedia.org/wiki/Rational _choice> Rev. 2009-11-27.

Weller, Marc 1994: Regional Peace-Keeping and International Enforcement: The Liberian Crisis, Cambridge: Cambridge University Press.

Yin, Robert K. 2003: Case Study Research: Design and Methods, 3rd ed., Thousand Oaks, London, New Delhi: Sage Publications.

Zangl, Bernhard/Zürn, Michael 2003: Frieden und Krieg: Sicherheit in der nationalen und postnationalen Konstellation, Frankfurt a. M.: Suhrkamp.

Zartman, William I. 1989: Ripe for Resolution, New York: Oxford University Press.

Zartman, William I. (ed.) 1995: Collapsed States: The Disintegration and Restoration of Legitimate Authority, Boulder, London: Lynne Rienner Publishers.

Index

175

Mehler, Andreas, 18, 125

Methodical considerations, 58-61

Miall, Hugh, 8, 9, 43, 44

Minin, Leonid, 84, 85

Most important sub-goals during peace implement-tation, 56, 57

Motives of war actors, 21, 23, 80-83

Movement of Democracy in Liberia (MODEL), 126-128, 130, 137, 138

Münkler, Herfried, 9, 21-23, 41

National Patriotic Front of Liberia – Central Revolutionary Council (NPFL-CRC), 112

National Patriotic Front of Liberia (NPFL), 70, 76, 80-84, 86, 89, 96-100, 102, 104, 106-109, 110-112, 122, 126

National Patriotic Party (NPP), 123, 125

National Patriotic Reconstruction Assembly (NPRA), 80

National Transitional Government of Liberia (NTGL), 129, 130, 140, 141

Natural resources, 2, 15, 21, 22, 24-26, 41-44, 46, 49, 56-58, 68, 69, 74, 75, 82-88, 90-96, 98, 109, 113, 122, 125-127, 129

Nature of the conflict, 14-18, 24-26, 41-44, 49, 50, 57, 58, 90-99, 111-113, 127-129

Negative peace, 8, 9, 12

Neighbouring states, 22, 41-44, 57, 58, 98, 99, 111, 112, 127, 128

New wars, 1, 2, 5, 6, 17, 18, 20-26, 35-37, 40, 41, 57, 58, 69-88

Nigeria, 112

Non-cooperation in the implementation phase, 30, 53-55, 105, 119, 138

Number of conflict parties, 42-44, 96, 97, 112, 113, 127-129

Number of peacekeepers, 47-49, 102, 103, 116, 117, 134-136

OAU peacekeepers, 102, 116

Obstructability, 95, 96

Olonisakin, Funmi, 74-79, 88, 90, 92, 96, 97, 99-103, 107, 108, 111, 114-116, 120-125

Operationalization, 15-18, 43-49, 55-57

'Operation Octopus', 89, 102

Peace consolidation, 5, 10-13, 24-26

Peace implementation, 1-3, 5-7, 11-18, 24-26, 29-64

Peace, 8-10, 13-18

People's Redemption Council (PRC), 68

www.ingramcontent.com/pod-product-compliance
Lightning Source LLC
Chambersburg PA
CBHW062148280526
45788CB00001B/349